QUALITY IMPROVEMENT IN EUROPEAN PUBLIC SERVICES

Concepts, Cases and Commentary

edited by
Christopher Pollitt
and Geert Bouckaert

SAGE Publications
London · Thousand Oaks · New Delhi

First published 1995

 SAGE Publications Ltd
6 Bonhill Street
London EC2A 4PU

SAGE Publications Inc
2455 Teller Road
Thousand Oaks, California 91320

SAGE Publications India Pvt Ltd
32, M-Block Market
Greater Kailash – I
New Delhi 110 048

British Library Cataloguing in Publication data

A catalogue record for this book is available
from the British Library.

ISBN 0 8039 7464 7
ISBN 0 8039 7465 5 (pbk)

Library of Congress catalog card number 95–068137

Typeset by Type Study, Scarborough
Printed in Great Britain by Biddles Ltd, Guildford, Surrey

Contents

PART THREE   OVERVIEW

Notes on the Contributors

Geert Bouckaert
Dr Bouckaert is engaged in research and teaching at the Public Management Centre, Katholieke Universiteit Leuven, Belgium. A holder of degrees in business engineering, political science, philosophy and social sciences, he has worked in the United States (State University of New York) as well as in Europe. The author of several books and articles, Dr Bouckaert is a specialist in issues of public sector quality and productivity. He is active in the International Institute of Administrative Sciences and the OECD.

Lucy Gaster
Lucy Gaster's concern for quality arose from her experience as a front-line manager in a London borough neighbourhood office during the 1980s and, before that, through her involvement in local community groups. Since 1990 she has been Research Fellow at the School for Advanced Urban Studies, University of Bristol. There she researches and teaches on a variety of aspects of public service delivery, including service quality, local democracy and decentralization.

Stephen Hanney
Dr Hanney is a Research Fellow in the Faculty of Social Sciences at Brunel University. Previously he taught at the Police Training College. His research has embraced performance measurement and quality issues across a range of public services and he is the co-author of a number of book, articles and reports.

Richard Joss
Having served in the police, Richard Joss has subsequently conducted large-scale academic research with the Centre for the Evaluation of Public Policy and Practice at Brunel University and also worked in the UK and overseas as an independent management consultant specializing in quality issues. He played a leading role in a major evaluation of TQM projects carried out for the Department of Health, and has worked extensively in both public and private sectors.

Helmut Klages
Dr Klages is Professor of Empirical Social Sciences at the Postgraduate School of Administrative Sciences in Speyer, Germany. He has designed and led several large empirical studies in the field of public sector modernization, leadership, motivation and determinants of employee behaviour in public organizations. Dr Klages was one of the main initiators of the nation-wide Speyer Quality Award.

Nico Mol
Dr Mol is Professor of Public Management at the Dutch Royal Military Academy and Associate Professor of Public Finance at the University of Twente.

Christopher Pollitt
After six years in the British Civil Service Dr Pollitt moved into academic life. Initially he worked at the innovative British Open University. From 1980 to 1988 he was Co-Editor of the journal *Public Administration*. Since 1990 he has been Professor of Government at Brunel University in West London. He is also Co-Director of the Centre for the Evaluation of Public Policy and Practice (CEPPP) and has carried out work for the European Commission, HM Treasury and the OECD. He is currently leading a major academic research project on the performance of autonomous public service delivery organizations.

Sylvie Trosa
For a number of years Dr Trosa was head of the evaluation division in the Department of Equipment in Paris. She was also Rapporteur Général for the Scientific Council for Evaluation, which reported to the Prime Minister of France. In 1993 she was seconded to the Cabinet Office in London and has also worked with the OECD and the Australian Department of Finance. Dr Trosa has published several articles and a book on performance-related pay.

Frans van Vught
Dr van Vught is Professor of Public Administration and Director of the Centre for Higher Education Policy Studies (CHEPS) at the University of Twente in the Netherlands. He has published many books and articles on futures, policy analysis and higher education policy.

Don F. Westerheijden
Dr Westerheidjen co-ordinates the group for research and the management of quality at the Centre for Higher Education Policy Studies (CHEPS) at the University of Twente in the Netherlands. He had edited and contributed to several books on quality assessment in higher education, and authored a number of articles in the same field. He acted as co-ordinator of the first round of the European Higher Education Advanced Training Course.

Hellen Westlund
Dr Westlund is Associate Professor at the School of Economics, University of Göteborg, Sweden. Her research has embraced the quality of consumer durables and convenience goods retailing as well as the quality of higher education. For many years she has also been a board member of a service industry company and a political representative on the Consumer Board of the City of Göteborg.

Introduction

Recognition of the need for this book grew out of a series of seminars financed by the UK Economic and Social Research Council and hosted by the Centre for the Evaluation of Public Policy and Practice at Brunel University. A range of European scholars with a specialist interest in public service quality were invited to attend these occasions and the present text owes a great deal to the insights thus generated. At an early stage we realized that, while the term 'quality' was increasingly fashionable among managers and politicians, it was also a potent source for conceptual and 'cultural' confusion. What is more, once these preliminary (but considerable) confusions had been cleared up, there seemed to be surprisingly little case study material available that was suitable for a European rather than a single-country (or even single-discipline) readership.

The plan and contents of the book follow rather directly from the above considerations. In Part One we begin by tackling the problem of defining quality (Chapter 1), noting that, far from being a merely semantic exercise, the choice (or lack of choice) of a particular concept of quality has significant political and organizational consequences. Then we move to the act of measurement (Chapter 2), without which 'quality' tends to remain a highly individualistic if not idiosyncratic entity. Though measurement can certainly be abused and overdone it is also the case that, so long as quality remains unmeasured, it will also be resistant to being planned, programmed, assured or otherwise consistently aimed for and achieved in those complex organizational settings that are so characteristic of our public services.

Part Two (Chapter 3 to 10) comprises a series of case studies, built around a set of common questions derived from the earlier analysis. These have been chosen to illustrate a range of different types of public services, using different technologies in different cultural and legal settings. They are drawn from France, Germany, the Netherlands, Sweden and the United Kingdom. The sequence of cases is roughly (but only roughly) from the more general and broad scope to the more detailed and local.

Part Three draws together an overview. Chapter 11 looks across the diverse set of experiences and attempts to draw out more general lessons in terms of fitting strategies for improvement to the purposes and circumstances of the organization in question. Chapter 12 offers some concluding reflections on the nature of service quality and the range of approaches to its improvement. While, on the one hand, considerable doubt is cast on the idea that there ever could be a single, universally applicable technique, certain patterns are distinguishable by which politicians, public managers, public service users and, more broadly, citizens may recognize the nature and potential of current initiatives.

Finally, as editors, we wish warmly to acknowledge the invaluable assistance given by the other members of the seminars, both those who have contributed chapters and those who gave their help in other ways. These include Valerie Beale, Marianne Bauer, David Burningham, Martin Buxton, Anna Coote, Yvonne Fortin, Mary Henkel, Luc Rouban, Charles Shaw and Jo Wright. Our thanks are also due to Diane Woodhead, who wrestled with a rainbow of software from all over Europe in order to generate the final text.

Christopher Pollitt
Brunel University, London

Geert Bouckaert
Katholieke Universiteit Leuven

PART ONE

DEFINITION AND OPERATIONALIZATION

1

Defining Quality

Christopher Pollitt and Geert Bouckaert

Preliminary remarks

'Quality': the word

'Quality' has become an immensely popular term where the organization of public services is concerned. It is on the lips of politicians, managers, professionals and citizens themselves. In health care, education, personal social services, fire services, the police and many other subsectors, commitments are being made to improve 'quality' and increase responsiveness to the 'customers' (clients/patients/students/users). Brochures and booklets are being issued, reports are being written, training courses are being delivered: 'quality' has become a central term in our contemporary rhetoric. It is scarcely conceivable that anyone would wish to argue against it: like virtue it seems unopposable.

Yet this dominance and pervasiveness should be enough to arouse our suspicions. Is everyone really pursuing the same objective, or do different groups have different things in mind when they adopt the 'quality' vocabulary? How and why did the term achieve such popularity? After all, as recently as the mid 1980s it was not particularly common in many of the settings in which it is now so fashionable.

To answer these questions, and to get beyond the words to practical matters of definition, measurement and implementation, requires careful analysis. It soon becomes apparent that there are many different meanings and different ways of operationalizing the concept. There are alternative approaches to measurement and implementation. There are difficult trade-offs and sensitive political judgements, some of these unavoidable. But there is also a growing body of practical experience about how to approach these issues in ways which recognize the distinctive contexts and values of the public services sector. This experience is not confined to one country or one service. In what follows we will interrogate this multi-conceptual, multi-national, multi-service body of knowledge and attempt to extract its key elements.

The case of total quality management (TQM)
To illustrate some of the foregoing observations it may be helpful to take a rapid first look at a particular case. We choose TQM as one well-known current approach to quality improvement. The aim here is *not* to offer an exhaustive analysis of TQM, but simply to show how careful and fundamental questions need to be asked before launching into large-scale adoption of such techniques within the public services sector. Broadly similar questions could be asked of most of the current management fashions, including benchmarking and re-engineering.

TQM was originally developed in the United States, was then widely and apparently successfully applied to Japanese manufacturing industry and was subsequently re-exported to the West. During the late 1970s and early 1980s it was extensively applied in manufacturing industry and gained fashionable status as one of the (alleged) secrets of Japanese business success. It percolated from manufacturing to the commercial services sector and eventually to public services. In the late 1980s, for example, TQM was officially embraced by the US federal civil service and, in the UK, a number of pilot TQM projects were launched in the National Health Service.

According to its literature the TQM approach usually includes at least the following elements:

1 A corporate perspective, frequently entailing the production of an organization-wide plan embodying specific quality goals.
2 The generation of real commitment and enthusiasm for quality all the way down the 'line' from top management to the 'shop floor'.
3 A transcendence of departmental and disciplinary boundaries (many quality problems typically arise *across* such intra-organizational boundaries).
4 A willingness to make a substantial investment in training.
5 A commitment to *continuous improvement*. TQM emphasizes an ongoing process rather than a once-for-all setting of quality standards.
6 An emphasis on avoiding mistakes or defects *before* they occur rather than correcting them retrospectively (and often expensively). This is encapsulated in the catch-phrase 'right first time'.

All of which sounds impressive. Again, who could oppose such an approach? Yet there are other ways of looking at the TQM phenomenon, and other questions that can be asked. First, for example, we can note the distinctly religious tone that surrounds much TQM work. It has become a domain of gurus (Ishikawa, Deming, Crosby), of fervently held beliefs, and of slogans. It resembles a managerial religion, one which happened to fit very well into Japanese culture and society. But how easily will it be to transplant the success of TQM to a quite different culture, and from manufacturing to services, and from for-profit business settings to public services which already possess their own strong and distinctive organizational cultures? At least one early evaluation has indicated that there are major problems, and has recommended significant modifications to TQM ideas to make them more appropriate for use in the context of a public health service (CEPPP, 1994).

One can also note, with a grain of scepticism, that the 'selling' of TQM seems to involve the profitable penetration of private sector consultants into the public sector. Just as the nineteenth-century spread of Christianity to the colonies was frequently closely bound up with commercial and imperial interests, so this new managerial religion has its own nexus of commercial and political advantage. Management consultants, sometimes aided and abetted by politicians and/or top management within the public sector, tend to want to focus attention on the question of 'How can we make this successful technique (TQM) work in this new setting?' But there are prior, more fundamental questions which are in danger of being overlooked. These include 'How do we construct a public sector which is ready to cope with the challenges of the next century?', and 'How do we create public organizations which are performing well, and which are both effective and accountable to the public, resulting in increased legitimacy for the public sector in particular and for the state and society in general?' These are not questions for the answers to which one would naturally or necessarily turn first to a for-profit management consultancy. Indeed, the answers to such questions may not involve TQM (or benchmarking, or re-engineering, or performance-related pay) at all. Or perhaps some selection of such techniques *will* figure as part of our answers, but only as a relatively minor and instrumental part, subservient to a broader philosophy and strategy that emphasizes the *distinctiveness* and *differences* of the public sector rather than presuming that the aim of public management is to ape private sector management in every possible way.

Even more philosophically, we may pause to consider the implications of the word 'total' in TQM. If a concept includes everything, it means nothing. It is necessary to *restrict* the meaning of a term to make it useful: only then can *discrimination* be made between one entity or issue and another. Apparently, however, TQM includes almost everything: resources (financial, human, material), products, organizations, procedures and so on. Furthermore it is hard to see what remaining difference there could be between management and TQM. All management thus becomes TQM. Is it possible to have at the conceptual level 'good' management which is different from TQM? The question then becomes: are the words 'total' or 'total quality' useful? Do they create some new meaning? The answer is that the 'T' in TQM appears to have a remarkably imperialistic purpose. It embraces:

1 the quantity and the quality of inputs, activities, outputs and effects;
2 the internal and external dimensions of an organization;
3 a *permanent* concern for the evolution of quality (TQM texts frequently emphasize the need for *continuous* improvement, over an indefinite time span).

To conclude this brief analysis of the TQM case we may point to the *absence* from the TQM vocabulary of many of the key concerns and concepts which have hitherto characterized debates about the provision of public services. Thus it is rare for the TQM literature to refer to 'citizens'. Its vocabulary is one of clients, customers, consumers and users. But there is a significant difference between these two clusters of concepts. It you pay taxes, or are arrested by the police, or go to prison, would you consider yourself as a client/customer/user of these services, or would you consider yourself as a citizen? A citizen can be defined as a concentration of rights and duties in the person of an individual, within a constitutional state, under the rule of law, and within a hierarchy of laws and regulations. The state supposedly exists to protect citizens and promote the general interest. A client is a concentration of needs and satisfactions of needs in an individual, within a market situation of supply and demand of goods and services, and within a hierarchy of needs, subject to the willingness to pay. A citizen is part of a social contract, whereas the client is part of a market contract. A 'client' is a part, but only a part, of the 'citizen'. The 'client' is also subordinate to the 'citizen'. There is a tendency for the so-called 'new public management' to turn this hierarchy upside down. Thus, for example, the key documents of the UK *Citizen's Charter* programme use the term 'citizen' rather infrequently, preferring terms denoting service consumer roles such as 'customer', 'passenger', 'tenant' and 'patient' (Pollitt, 1994).

 TQM remains silent on such issues and thus, implicitly, downgrades the traditional (and hard-won) language of the duties and rights of citizenship. This is perhaps not surprising, considering the contexts in which TQM was developed. It would be unreasonable to criticize a management technique for failing to address issues which it was never designed to address. It is entirely reasonable, however, to ask how these issues and concerns *are* going to be addressed if techniques such as TQM are going to be used on a large scale within the public service sector.

Background: the rise of 'quality'
Having briefly considered the case of TQM we now return to our broader investigation of the term 'quality' and its rapid rise to popularity. Several developments came together to propel 'quality' to the forefront. One was largely internal to the public services, namely the intensification of pressure for economy and efficiency. An almost universal feature of public service life from the late 1970s, this pressure can be traced to the global economic upheavals following the oil price rises of 1973 and 1979. The end of the long economic boom and the realization that demographic and technological factors were steadily pushing up expenditures in huge programmes such as pensions and health care led Western governments to seek new ways to streamline public service delivery. Phrases such as 'cost improvements', 'performance indicators' and 'running cost efficiency gains' became common. Everywhere pressures were felt to reduce staff and rationalize the purchase of organizational inputs. Often citizen entitlements to benefits or services were narrowed, or charges were introduced, or the indexing of payments was weakened.

This drive for economy and efficiency soon exhibited its own limitations. From the perspective of many of the staff providing public services it could never be a prime motivator. These were people devoted to service *improvements* (doctors, teachers, nurses, librarians and so on) and a diet of pure economy was insufficiently nourishing. In a number of services there was evidence of a serious fall in morale. Nor were economy and efficiency (however necessary) adequate rallying cries for the citizens who used these services. They, too, wanted improvements, choices, alternatives. 'Quality' seemed the ideal concept to fill the gap, especially since, outside the public sector, the business world appeared to have developed significant new techniques (such as TQM) for achieving quality improvements. Making 'quality' a main objective could help restore the morale of staff, reassure citizens anxious about the threatened decline of their basic public services, and provide politicians with a new set of slogans and rallying cries. Of course quality improvement did not *replace* the drive for economy, but rather complemented it. It held out the promise of squaring the circle: with these new techniques, perhaps the cost of public services could be lowered whilst at the same time the satisfaction of their users could be raised.

Interestingly, the rhetorical bubble of 'quality' may be about to burst. At the time of writing we are beginning to encounter managers who are consciously moving their vocabularies away from 'quality', partly because of a sense that recently the term has been overused and devalued, and partly because they wish to avoid the implication that quality is something separate from other management functions. It has been suggested to us that 'good business practice' is a more useful, generic term because it includes quality concerns but also embraces equally important issues such as developing a clear strategy, exercising appropriate budgetary controls and practising good business ethics.

The context for quality improvement: differences within Western Europe

The position of public services, indeed of the whole relationship between citizens and the state apparatus, differs from country to country. Some of the particular differences carry significant implications for notions of public service 'quality'. On continental Europe a basic concern is the rule of law and the positions of the citizen. Respect for the law and protections of the citizen are more important than the mere search for quality in a product or service. This difference of emphasis or point of departure can be seen in the citizens' charters produced in the UK (1991), France (1992) and Belgium (1992). All purport to deal with the quality of public services, but whereas the UK charter says and does little to alter the status of the citizen under the law this is very much the starting point for the French *Chartes des Services Publics*. The Belgian *Charte de l'Utilisateur des Services Publics* is different again, putting its stress on the balance of duties between state and citizen. In these continental charters the point of departure is not so much the product or the service for the customer as the participation of citizens in the planning and production of services. There is little or no willingness to dilute the rule of law in order to gain some so-called quality improvement in a product or service.

In the UK, by contrast, the concept of 'the state' has never been so prominent, and the system of administrative law is perhaps less well developed than in those continental states such as France and Germany which evolved from absolute monarchies. These historically rooted differences exhibit themselves in a number of ways, not least in the weaker (or at least more diffuse) notion of citizenship which is in play within the UK political system (Prior et al., 1993: 5–6). During the 1980s and early 1990s neo-liberal Conservative administrations were therefore able to redescribe major public services such as health care and education by using the private sector, market-oriented language of 'customers', 'providers' and 'contracts'. Thus, in the UK, there has been a tendency to try to divorce quality improvement activities from consideration of the politician/citizen relationship. Quality improvement has been portrayed as essentially an unpolitical question of 'good management', in which public service administrators are expected to study private sector market relationships and to treat the users of their services not as citizens but as 'customers' or 'consumers'. Indeed, the government has taken considerable steps to try to ensure that its quality improvement initiatives do *not* create new legal rights, and that the quality specifications embodied in public service contracts and service agreements are *not* actionable in the courts.

It would be inaccurate, however, to portray the UK experience as unique and those of all the continental European states as essentially similar. The true picture is more complicated and includes both significant differences *between* continental states (see Chapters 4 and 5 for example) *and* some broad trends which have affected both the UK and the continental states. One of these trends is worthy of immediate mention: we refer to the shift from 'traditional' towards 'new' relationships in respect of the shaping of public services. The traditional relationships are essentially bureaucratic and hierarchical, the new ones more pluralistic. Traditionally the political leaders determine what service is to be provided, on what terms and to whom, and bureaucrats and professionals subsequently organize and deliver that service. Standards and procedures are determined internally, usually by the bureaucrats and professionals, without too much political interference. The role of the citizens is mainly passive: to apply and wait to see if they are eligible, or to turn up when summoned.

In the new relationships which have been developing throughout Europe (though at different speeds and with many variances of detail) the range of actors *institutionally* involved in the production, delivery and evaluation of public services has increased. Citizen-users are consulted about service provision in a wide variety of ways (user advisory panels or councils, consultative committees, satisfaction surveys and so on). This may begin with a one-off survey to establish how satisfied users are with an existing service. It soon develops into regular surveys and, beyond that, into a realization by the state authorities that users may have an important role to play in defining quality standards or even the format and desirability of new types of service. The chapters that follow contain many examples of such institutionalized involvement by users.

Citizen-users are not the only newcomers to the business of standard setting and quality assurance. The blurring of roles between service providers and service consumers has been paralleled by role shifts *within* provider organizations. Managers and administrators have extended their influence over what were formerly the territories of single professions (see e.g. Pollitt, 1993). Politicians, attracted by the salience of quality issues (for which they have themselves been partly responsible), have begun to pay more attention to how service quality is measured and publicized. In the introduction to the UK *Citizen's Charter* the Prime Minister declared that it was a personal ambition of his 'to make public services answer better the wishes of their users and to raise their quality overall' (Prime Minister, 1991: 2).

Ultimately such 'new relationships' raise fundamental questions about democratic participation and political legitimacy. Although these deeper questions of democratic theory and practice are not the prime focus of the book they are a vital and somewhat neglected dimension of the search for 'quality'. We will refer to them at a number of points, and return to consider them in a more comprehensive way in the final chapter.

Having sketched the rhetorical and international context we can now begin the task of *defining* the subtle and elusive concept of 'quality'.

Quality as a feature of systems

Goods and services

Some of the best-known quality improvement techniques were originally developed to tackle the private sector production of goods for profit. The first generation of techniques tended to focus on 'mistakes' – on the percentage of defective products rolling off the end of the production line. Such techniques were therefore principally concerned with quality as 'fitness for use', where the producer, drawing on production expertise, determined what was 'fit' and what was not.

This simple notion was subsequently developed along two dimensions. First, it was realized that 'fitness' needed to be interpreted in a broad way. 'Unfitness' might be the function of some non-technical feature of the product, for example that it was regarded as ugly or unfashionable, or that it was late in delivery, or that the after-sales service was poor. Thus an electric drill might 'work' quite well, but unless it was attractively designed, delivered to retailers on time and backed up by good after-sales service, it was not a 'quality product'. Secondly, manufacturers realized that the producer did not always know best – that 'fitness' needed to be determined by those using the products rather than those making them. The producers frequently *thought* they knew what was wanted, but unless they talked to their customers, continuously and systematically, they might easily be mistaken.

The techniques which manufacturers developed to deal with these issues were often impressive in their thoroughness. Yet there are several reasons why they (and some of their underlying concepts) are likely to prove less appropriate for many public services.

First, as has been widely noted, services are unlike goods in that quality cannot be 'designed in' in quite the same way. A service cannot be produced, checked, stored and then brought out, fresh in its packaging, when the customer appears. Services are created on the spot: they are consumed as they are produced, and cannot be stored.

Furthermore, while some services are capable of being standardized, many others are not (or at least, not yet). Each electric drill is the same. But no one school lesson is identical with another and neither are any two appendectomies or social worker home visits. Indeed, the services concerned employ professionals and grant them considerable discretion precisely so that they will be able to vary the service they deliver according to their judgements about a host of local and particular circumstances. This feature of services also poses problems for quality improvement approaches which depend on the very precise specification of activities *in advance*.

This last point can be taken further. The outcomes of some service interactions depend as much on the reaction of the user as they do on the behaviour of the provider. The school child has to want to learn. The patient has to want to get well. The ex-criminal, on probation, has to be determined not to fall back into criminal activity. If such *willingness* and *responsiveness* is entirely absent, the service may 'fail', despite the best possible efforts of the service provider. Thus services of this type have been termed examples of *co-production*, where both user and provider play important parts in 'producing' the outcomes. It follows from this that scope for providers to 'design quality in' in advance is likely to be seriously limited. The very definition of quality will be co-produced.

Public and private
According to the arguments in the previous subsection, there are important differences between goods and services. There are, however, *further* distinctions which make *public* services (or at least most of them) different from private sector services (or at least most of them). In a private sector commercial market the feedback links between seller/producer and customer/user are very direct, and serve constantly to remind the producer of the importance of meeting consumer wants. If sales decline that is an immediate indication that something is wrong. Since the producer's revenue usually declines as the sales decline this 'something' cannot for long be ignored. The possibility that the quality is too low for the price of the service is one of the things that demands immediate investigation. Perhaps another, rival producer has found a way of offering the same quality at a lower price, or a higher-quality service at the same price. Either way, the first producer gets early feedback that something is going wrong, and faces immediate loss of revenue if appropriate remedial actions are not identified and taken.

In public services, feedback on quality is much less forceful. To begin with, the service is frequently provided free at the point of use, or at least at a charge which is only weakly related to costs (because it is subsidized from taxation). Because of this many public services are faced with the problem of limiting demand (rationing). A fall in demand can actually be a relief: less pressure, more time for professional development, research or leisure, little or no reduction in budget. An increase in demand, by contrast, may be very unwelcome, because it means more pressure on staff and facilities but probably no increase in budget (or only a disproportionately small one). It is only in recent years that changes in budgeting practices have begun to lessen these 'perverse incentives' by relating budgets to workloads or performance.

The phenomenon of 'excess' demand which leads to queues and rationing decreases the motivation to improve quality in other ways too. If one customer dislikes the service and goes elsewhere there is usually another one waiting in the queue. Large-scale desertion ('exit') may be unlikely because the public provider occupies a monopolistic or oligopolistic position (there are few if any alternative services to exit *to*). This restriction on behaviour is, of course, likely to be felt most acutely by low-income consumers. Trapped in a monopolistic system which provides them with essentials such as health care or education or social security benefits, such consumers often form very low expectations for service quality. To put it bluntly, they get used to low standards and so do the service providers.

Two further points about 'publicness' deserve mention. The first is that some public services are actually supplied *against* the wishes of the immediate 'user' because they are part of the control apparatus of the state. Following other authors (Stewart, 1992) we term these *social ordering* services because they are concerned with maintaining the general social order. Prison and police services fall into this category, as do certain aspects of the personal social services (social workers administering child care orders, probation services and so on) and various types of inspectorate (pollution, weights and measures). In a medium-sized country these services affect millions of citizens, yet they have little parallel in the literature on quality in the commercial sector. They raise an interesting point concerning the definition of quality. In an ordinary service such as a restaurant one would naturally look to the customer for information as to whether acceptable quality standards were being achieved. Yet to base policing standards on what the criminals say, or pollution control standards on what the polluters want, is obviously perverse. These social ordering functions operate, rather, to standards which are (implicitly at least) set by their acceptability to society as a whole. Given the size and diversity of most societies the problem of ascertaining what that acceptable standard may be is obviously hugely more complex than the equivalent problem for a restaurant.

Finally there is the related point that several of the public service professions (medicine, teaching, social work) have long operated with certain concepts of social 'need' which are derived more from the collective purposes of their organizations or professions than from individual consumer 'wants'. Doctors will tell mothers that their children 'need' vaccinations; teachers will explain to parents that their child 'needs' a remedial class in some subject; professional firemen may insist that a building meets a certain standard in respect to the risk of fire; social workers may employ a particular concept of a 'normal' or 'functional' family in suggesting preferred behaviours to their clients. These 'needs' may (or may not) be in direct contra-diction with the personal wishes of the citizen concerned. Or they may function in a situation where the service user is in some way incapacitated and/or unable to articulate his or her own wants effectively (for example an elderly mentally ill person, a baby, future generations).

Each of these features makes the business of defining and operationalizing quality more challenging and complex than in the proverbial supermarket. They have implications for measurement, training, monitoring and evaluation. The case studies we will introduce in later chapters well illustrate this complexity.

Levels of quality

The focus on 'quality' in the public sector can be situated at three levels: the micro, the meso and the macro levels of society.

Micro-quality is an internal quality concept which applies to the interrelationships of the top, middle and base of an organization. From an internal perspective an important purpose is to increase the quality of working life for staff by paying attention to their needs, aspirations and creativity. The underlying assumption is that contented and committed staff will work more effectively. Thus the ultimate purpose is to improve the organization's performance. For example, one method is to set up quality circles (QCs). A further assumption here (as in a number of recent quality improvement techniques) is that there can be a harmony of interests between the owners or top managers and the various other occupational groups within the organization. Without wishing to take the cynical view that such harmony is *never* attainable, it would be foolish not to recognize that there is a long and distinguished line of organizational sociology testifying to the fact that interests frequently conflict within modern organizations (e.g. Alvesson, 1987). Thus an ideological perversion of contemporary 'human resources management' may be for top management to use HRM in such a way as subtly to manipulate rank and file staff. When the employer begins to use the objective of quality improvement to demand 'commitment' (Storey, 1989) and 'positive thinking' as well as mere compliance, the echoes of George Orwell's Big Brother are disturbingly loud (Orwell, 1949).

Meso-quality is an external quality concept which applies to the relationship between producer and consumer, or supply and demand, or provider and user. The general aim is to increase the external quality of the service by paying more attention to those on the demand side. One method is to focus on total quality management (Crosby, 1988; Deming, 1986; Juran, 1988). The assumption here is that of an essential harmony of interests between the service providers and the public. If the organization pays continuous, detailed attention to what the consumer wants, business will prosper. The ideological perversion may therefore be to (ab)use this principle of consumer involvement by operationalizing it in such a way as to permit manipulation of the consumer by the technocrats or professionals. Thus (for example) under the guise of professional advice an insurance broker may persuade clients to take out more insurance than they really need, or a doctor may encourage a patient to undergo investigations or interventions that are medically unnecessary, because they bring more business to his/her hospital or practice.

Macro-quality is a generic system concept which applies to the relationship between a public service and the citizenry, and to the relationship between the state and civil society. The fundamental concern is the improvement of the quality of life in society, including within that broad concept the quality of citizen/state relations. This involves focusing on societal trade-offs (where and where not to spend government money) taking 'externalities' into account. The achievement of quality in this macro sense is likely to re-establish the public's trust not only in the particular public services concerned but also more broadly in the state and system of governance. In other words the improvement of macro-quality is expected to increase what political scientists refer to as the *legitimacy* of a particular system or regime. A popular recent approach to this has been to develop citizens' charters. In a sense these may be seen as Rousseauian attempts to renew the social contracts between rulers and ruled. The possible ideological perversion here is fairly obvious: charters could be used as ways of creating favourable publicity whilst actually channelling citizen discontent into management-designed procedures and increasing centralized state control over standards. In the UK, for example, there has already been an example of top management in a university strongly criticizing dissatisfied students because they approached the mass media rather than using the internal channels for dissent provided by the *Student's Charter*. Charters may also be used to focus public attention on measured increases in the minimum standards for a service, disguising the fact that average standards may be falling (Pollitt, 1994).

The main focus of this book will be on the meso level. We immediately acknowledge, however, that the three levels are connected and substantially interdependent. There will therefore be occasions on which reference will be made to both macro and micro levels.

A multi-polar concept of quality

Two major perspectives on quality

To simplify, there seem to be two major points of view. First, there is a producer or provider point of view in which quality is related to output and where conformance to predetermined requirements is the dominant idea. Of course, producers are not internally homogeneous, so there may be internal tensions over who is to determine the requirements for output. In some professionalized public services the tension is currently between managers and professionals (see e.g. Pollitt, 1993). Furthermore, there may be a further internal tension between output-focused definitions of quality and process-focused definitions of quality. Typically, for example, professional groups may prefer relatively informal, process-oriented standards, policed by the professional peer group, whereas managers prefer quantified output measures which are embodied in performance indicators that senior management can monitor. Nevertheless, despite these frequently occurring internal complications, we may define *producer quality* as:

> the intrinsic features of the good or service itself, as seen by those producing it.

Secondly, however, there is a consumer viewpoint on quality. This *user quality* we may define as:

> the quality of the good or service as it is perceived by the user.

It should immediately be pointed out that the user may or may not value (or even notice) the features or attributes which were deemed to constitute 'quality' by the producer. Many organizations have discovered, when they research users' wants, that they had previously possessed only a highly imperfect picture of what their users actually wanted. Professional service providers, in particular, may develop an exaggerated or poorly calibrated assessment of the degree to which they understand their clients' wishes and aspirations.

User quality thus pertains to the effects (outcomes) of the goods or services which are consumed – to their utility, the capacity to satisfy wants, their fitness for purpose – all from the user's, not the producer's point of view. To the extent that these effects are positive – *or believed to be positive* – the user will be satisfied. The emphasis here is vital: it is the *belief or perception* that matters rather than any 'objective facts' about the situation. Perhaps car A *does* have greater reliability than car B (as measured by independent observers). Nevertheless, a user of car A who *believes* that car B, belonging to their neighbour, is more reliable, is likely to be dissatisfied with car A. This is an example of individual perceptions, but the point also applies to perceptions shared within a particular socio-economic, occupational or ethnic group. Thus it is entirely possible for different groups to experience differing levels of satisfaction from what appears to outsiders to be exactly the same service! In several mass public services this is a point of considerable importance. Survey evidence has shown, for example, that professional middle class users may sometimes be less satisfied with the UK National Health Service than users in the lower socio-economic groups.

Thus *satisfaction* (or dissatisfaction) is the result of the confrontation of expectations (individual or collective) and perceived quality. If the perceived quality of a service was medium (a concert, for example) but the expectations had been very high, there will be dissatisfaction. On the other hand, if prior expectations had been very low then even quite a poor service may result in user satisfaction. This can open up a manipulative opportunity for politicians and/or public service producers: logically they can increase satisfaction (or, at least, reduce dissatisfaction) either by raising the perceived quality of services *or by lowering public expectations*.

To some extent a lowering of expectations is exactly what has been happening during the 1980s in a number of countries – at least on the level of macro-quality. Governments (especially but not exclusively those of the 'new right') have stressed that the welfare state is becoming too expensive, and that it has to be restricted. Thus benefit categories have been narrowed, co-payments increased, pension entitlement ages raised, and so on. The message has been that the public had been expecting too much, and that they must now be 'realistic'.

Much of the discussion in this subsection applies to private sector services as well as public. However, the factors special to the public sector (see earlier) also play a part. We will mention only two here. First, there is the absence of market-type competition across considerable areas of the public service sector. This is important because it may restrict the development of high expectations by users – because they have little with which to compare the service they are receiving (unless they use the same services in other countries, which, of course, is increasingly beginning to happen). Absence of competition may also remove the incentive for producers to find out exactly what their users want, since the users have no effective power of 'exit'. It is not surprising, therefore, that some monopoly or near-monopoly public services have developed in a producer-dominated way.

The second special feature of the public services is the role of governments. In a sense they blur the producer/user distinction, because they represent both. They 'own' and finance the services in question (and frequently employ most or all of the staff delivering them). Yet they also democratically represent the users. This dualism can and occasionally does result in somewhat schizophrenic behaviour on the part of governments. On the one hand they will seek to define very closely the maximum that will be on offer (producer quality), to restrict public expectations and to economize (in order to please bankers and taxpayers). On the other hand they will put pressure on public service organizations to be more responsive to users, to adhere to citizens' charters, to raise quality and so on (in order to please the service users who elect them, and to enhance the legitimacy of the system).

Defining quality: concluding remarks
By this stage in the argument it will be clear why the definition of quality is such a difficult matter. For, far from being just some technical characteristic, inherent in the product or service, the notion of quality also embraces the *values* or utilities which those producing the service, consuming it or being otherwise affected by it attribute to these characteristics. Since different individuals and groups may choose different characteristics as the most important ones for them, quality is, at base, inescapably political and social as well as technical. If the firm producing a car wants it to meet environmental legislation, half the potential drivers most want it to be fast and the other half most want it to be cheap, then negotiations, compromises and power relationships become the order of the day. Should the firm use advertising to try to alter user expectations, so that environmental factors become a larger component in users' satisfaction? Should it make several different types of car (smaller production runs, therefore probably more expensive), each for its own group of users? Should it lobby the government to get some relaxation of environmental requirements? These complexities may be multiplied several-fold if, instead of a car, we substitute the education of a child or a programme of care for a frail and mentally impaired elderly person.

It follows from this that any worthwhile definition of quality will need to say something about *whose* values are to be counted, and will also have to allow for the fact that quality is likely to be a matter of degree (and compromise or trade-off), not the simple presence or absence of some single property. Ideally it should also embrace the possibility that, as values, experiences and expectations change, so will quality standards. What was acceptable quality 20 years ago may well be unacceptable today – for social as well as technological reasons. In this sense the 'continuous improvement' proclaimed as a goal by TQM may be simply the counterpart of continuously rising user expectations.

We are left, therefore, with a concept that is both subtle and dynamic. Each purpose held by each group of users (or producers) can have its own 'quality'. The expectations against which (dis)satisfaction is generated can move up or down over time. 'Quality' seems to dissolve into a multitude of separate attributes, each one more or less important for this or that group among the producers or users. To find some way of measuring such an elusive entity is both essential and enormously challenging. The next chapter discusses this challenge.

2
Measuring Quality

Geert Bouckaert

For a long time, the activity of measurement has been considered a purely technical problem which does not really affect the functioning of organizations. Measurement is just like taking the temperature of the managerial body, it is said – like accountants counting money. This idea of measurement as a neutral activity is withering away. Measurement of quality is not considered to be objective or neutral any more. For example, in analysing waiting times in hospitals Hart (1994) noticed that this measurement activity triggered a broader quality improvement effort. Even walking around with the measurement sheets was sufficient stimulus to affect the behaviour of those being measured. The preceding chapter discussed the conceptual framework, and suggested some of the range of problems in operationalizing these concepts. Bringing in the idea of subjectivity makes it even more complex. In a sense the status of measurement is decreasing as its objective flavour is vanishing. Finally, the confrontation of a conceptually controversial and subjective measure with a norm or standard brings together a wide range of problems one may encounter in measurement. Norms and standards are related to expectations, which are even more complex than subjective measures!

Criteria for good measurement

In general, measurement is a condition for meaningful management (Bouckaert, 1991, 1993). For measurement to be meaningful to management the activity of measurement has to be valid and reliable, functional and legitimate. Measurement is more than inventing technically sound measures, collecting data, processing these data and distributing the information. Three sets of conditions have to be satisfied.

Validity and reliability: quality of measuring
Technically, quality measures have to possess certain inner features. Two major criteria for the soundness of measures are validity and

reliability. A valid quality measure is sound, cogent and convincing, and reveals what it professes to reveal. A reliable measure has stability in place and time. Reliable measures are therefore repeatable in place and time, transparent, precise and comprehensive. Repeatability is crucial for comparisons in time, between places, and with standards and norms. The length of a road is a reliable measure because it can be measured many times and the answer should always turn out to be the same number of metres. It could be less valid as a measure for maintenance if the surface rather than the length is crucial. The number of potholes in a road can be a reliable quality measure, if a pothole is well defined, because it is possible for different persons to count them and always come to the same result. Yet, this may be a less valid measure since it says nothing about the size of the potholes. A distribution of size and numbers of potholes may be a valid and reliable set of measures. Hatry et al. (1992) refer to the 'roughometer' as a tool to measure potholes as indicators of the quality of streets.

Functionality versus dysfunctionality
It is not sufficient that measures are technically sound. Individuals and organizations measure in order (for example) to be able to establish their location on a map of progress, or compare themselves with others. Measurement has to support the purpose of the organization. Dysfunctional measures may be valid and reliable, but endanger or inhibit achievement of the organization's objectives. In social services, measuring the output as the number of closed cases may result in closing cases without full regard for the correctness of the solution. Although the number of closed cases is a valid and reliable measure, it may result in dysfunctional effects. Shifting to the number of *correctly* closed cases results again in a valid and reliable measure. Yet, this too may become dysfunctional for the social service because the social workers may then be tempted to encourage easy cases to come in and discourage the difficult cases which are really in need of the service. The solution here could be to use the number of correctly closed cases and weight this number for the degree of difficulty of the cases (Bouckaert, 1995).

The functionality of a measure may depend on different elements. For example:

1 Appropriate timing for distribution of information may be crucial. Late information is more likely to be ignored.
2 Short-term or long-term focus for interpretation may affect the

potential for action and dynamism. Measures should stimulate continuous improvement.

3 Hierarchies of measures and their aggregations could affect the degree of functionality. Aggregating measures at a higher level wipes out both the best and worst practices and reduces the number of observations going beyond a benchmark.

4 Proliferation of information is crucial in providing motivation, improvement and accountability. The distribution of information should be determined by an organizational learning strategy rather than old-fashioned bureaucratic conventions such as 'need to know'.

5 A cost–benefit analysis should be conducted for each measurement system. Too high a cost compared with the benefit of having the information may cause dysfunctions.

6 The size of the measurement system should be manageable and transparent. Too big a system invites self-serving strategies in the measurement system and creates the potential for selective perceptions which may result in conflicting organizational purposes.

Legitimacy and ownership

It is possible for a quality measurement system to consist of valid and reliable measures, and for the system to possess the potential to support the healthy functioning of the organization. Yet the measurement system, which consists of the measures themselves and the procedures for collecting data, processing data and distributing this information, may still not be working as it should. This will happen to the extent that the system is mistrusted or disowned by those who have to use it. Ownership and legitimacy should be defined in a broad sense. Citizens and customers, as well as provider staff, can be asked what measures they think should be used to assess quality. Getting citizens, professionals and civil servants jointly involved in developing the measurement system increases the chances that quality measurement will be taken seriously and will be effective.

Who measures?

Knowledge through measurement is a source of power within and beyond the organization. Therefore it is important to know who measures. Control of the measurement system is frequently related to the broader distribution of power within that organization. Thus in a technocratic organization, a professional, technical elite will design

Table 2.1 *Result of producer/consumer information disequilibrium*

| | | Producer standards | |
		Available	Not available
Consumer perception	Good	Agree or disagree	Consumer domination
	Bad	Producer domination	Searching

and use the measurement system to serve their own interests. In a representative democracy, leading policy-makers (ministers and their most senior advisers) will exert a dominant influence over information flows. In a competitive market, or a system of direct democracy, customers or citizens will have the clout to ensure that information relevant to *their* decisions is collected and made available.

Of course, these are models or ideal types. The real world is usually more complicated. Nevertheless, a major current theoretical *and* practical issue in the public services sector is whether there may be an information disequilibrium or asymmetry between consumer and producer. Consumers may have a good perception of what the service is and should be, or not. The producers may have good technical standards for what the service is and should be, or not. Four positions are possible (see Table 2.1):

1 If both have information, they may agree or disagree, which puts the consumer in a position to bargain and negotiate (for example, on school boards). This is sometimes referred to as the *voice* option.
2 If both have bad information, this may put the consumer in a searching position (for example, subsidies and grants for restoring buildings in an ambiguous legislative framework).
3 If consumers do have good information but producers do not, this may put consumers in a position to convince and to defend their case; this is also a type of voice option (for example, informed self-help groups *vis-à-vis* professional social counselling).
4 If producers have good information and consumers do not, this will put the consumers in a position where trust and loyalty, or exit, are the only options (for example, does a patient trust an expert neuro-surgeon, or look for another one, or avoid treatment?).

This analysis assumes that all stakeholders have good data processing capacity. Unless there are citizen watch groups, or customer groups,

Table 2.2   *Differentiation in behaviour due to an information disequilibrium between producers and consumers*

| | | Producer standards | |
		Available	Not available
Consumer perception	Good	Bargain or negotiate	Convince
	Bad	Trust or exit	Search

citizens and customers are usually in a weak position. Their capacity to *process* (sometimes complex) data may be inferior to that of providers because the former do not have the resources to invest in training, they lack the know-how, they are informed too late about changes in circumstances and so on. This gives a systematic and significant advantage to the provider. Improving monitoring systems and accountability mechanisms may enhance the process of information provision. However, even with good feedback to the public domain there will still remain certain categories of service user who have information processing difficulties, such as children, the mentally ill or the elderly.

In this setting it is assumed that there are only two stakeholders. This is not necessarily the case. Multi-stakeholder positions and a multi-interest focus complicate the picture. Nevertheless, coalitions or cross-alliances are possible. This influences the behaviour of the stakeholders involved (see Table 2.2).

There are numerous taxonomies based on features of the environmental setting of the service, the activities producing these goods or services, or the output. All these classifications have implications for differences in producer/consumer relationships, the information distribution and the related balance of power. Each tends to produce a distinctive pattern of behaviour by each of the main actors.

The following list, which is not comprehensive, provides some criteria according to which quality measurement systems may differ:

1 Divisible (passport delivery) versus indivisible (security): it will be easier for divisible goods and services to differentiate between different categories of customers.
2 Tangible (garbage collection) versus intangible (counselling): visibility and countability have an impact on quality assessment.
3 Products (storable goods) versus services (unstorable, such as relational counselling): goods are usually more visible, standardizable and countable than services.

4 Inspection goods (raw materials, stationery: very tangible quality) versus experience goods (consulting, auditing, debt collection, weather forecasting: customers extrapolate their experience and suppliers accumulate goodwill) versus trust goods (administration of justice by courts, armed forces, public welfare systems, general public administration, diplomatic services: quality cannot even be assessed by experience (Blankart, 1987).

5 Production goods (outputs and outcomes are visible: street cleaning) versus procedure goods (outputs are visible and outcomes are not: courts, training of the military in peacetime) versus craft organizations (output is not visible, outcome is visible: forest rangers) versus coping organizations (neither output nor outcome is visible: schools) (Wilson, 1989).

6 Free (library) versus not free at the point of use (defence): this freedom influences perceptions and expectations.

7 Voluntarily consumed (symphony orchestra) versus compulsory (prison): this dimension also influenced perceptions and expectations.

8 Continuous contact (training) versus rarely or episodically used (registering birth, marriage, death): this is influenced by the level of involvement of actors.

9 Aims at behavioural change (AIDS campaigns) or does not so aim (tax collection).

10 Short-term consequence (green space maintenance) versus long-term consequence (equipment): time perspectives of different actors may be in conflict.

Different tactics and strategies will have to be developed to strengthen the position of users according to which category they occupy within this list.

The fine detail of data collection and processing can have much wider significance. For example there may be automatic collection and processing of data. It is possible to register output and quality when computer terminals are logged on, when files are opened, when data are added to files (such as how long it took to finish and close a customer file). Informatics, one-stop reorganization of working procedures, and central data processing through a network, facilitate measuring volumes and quality (waiting time, bottle-necks, availability of the service, downtime of the system and so on). This may be used in car licence registering agencies, for example. Alternatively it is possible that low-level clerical personnel are collecting or processing data. They may have a low status in the organization, be poorly paid, work under the responsibility of high-status people, and not always have the capacity or the confidence to speak up if something goes wrong. In some hospitals poorly trained staff with a high turnover may have to decipher what doctors or nurses have scribbled on a medical record card, in order to input data to a computer. Professionals may dominate the measurement system and the related managerial information. Another possibility is that customers themselves will input the data.

One case study seemed to show that, in maternity units, mothers were better file keepers than their hospitals (Williamson, 1992). Customers have a direct stake in keeping files in order, complete, updated, correct and available.

Types of quality measure

The previous section warns that the acquisition of quality measures which are valid, reliable, functional and widely regarded as legitimate will be a formidable task. For what will be needed – at least on an ideal level – will be a measure which can capture the perceptions of possibly many different service dimensions (such as speed, reliability, friendliness) held by several different groups (producers, users and so on).

According to some scholars the ideal measurement system will somehow enable decision-makers to translate these values into a common denominator which will allow all the different judgements along all the different dimensions to be averaged or traded off against each other, so that an overall 'balance sheet' or single quality index can be arrived at. For example, in measuring the total performance of refuse collection Hatry and Fisk (1971) suggested a mixed measure consisting of volume of refuse collected (tons), cost of collection (US$), producer-defined quality (measured by trained observers on a scale from one for very dirty to four for very clean and citizen-defined quality (measured by citizen satisfaction as a percentage of the population).

It has always been a human ambition to grasp the complexity of reality and reduce it to understandable dimensions. Quality, as an example of this complexity, is also subject to this desire. The major dangers in reduction to a single index are twofold. First, it creates a situation which is not at all transparent. The different dimensions are not visible and the hidden and implicit weights, or the choice of the weights, gives extensive power to the producers and professionals. Secondly, it also allows for dimensions to be compensated. Quality (as satisfaction) may be traded off against cost and result in what is apparently a good 'score' on the combined measure, although quality may have a very low score.

Literature and practice suggest that there have been a succession of general approaches to the quality–performance relationship. One solution is simply to *assume* that quality is equal and constant if services have to be compared. If this is the case, quality should not be measured explicitly at all since it will not provide a differentiating answer. Thus comparison is made of the *quantities* of output only. Some studies in the 1960s took this position (Ross and Burkhead, 1974). Bradford et al. (1969: 188–9) developed time series for education, health, police, fire services and welfare organizations. They recognized the problem of possible changes in quality, which partly result in cost increases. Yet, they explicitly ignored this improvement in quality, for practical and operational reasons.

A second answer is not to count output below a certain level of quality. If perceived deficient by a quality control check this output will be sent back to the production line and not counted (Hatry, 1979: 37). Thus measured performance will automatically exclude those outputs which fail the minimum quality threshold.

A third answer is to select those organizations with a similar output quality. A criterion is determined, quality is measured, and only those observations are selected with an (approximately) equal quality for an analysis of a homogeneous cluster (Ammons, 1984: 50–84). Ammons, in his comparison of 14 cities with high-quality services, discusses the relevance of the quality of services to their productivity. The 14 cities are selected because of their high quality standards in seven services: police (less than national average rate of motor vehicle thefts); fire (public protection classification of four or better); refuse collection (twice-a-week back-door residential collection); streets (pavements and kerb index of 80 per cent or greater); library (per capita circulation of 4.5 or greater); parks and recreation (at least one lighted municipal tennis court per 5,000 population); financial administration (recipient of Municipal Finance Officers Association Certificate of Conformance for Financial Reporting). This creates a practice cluster which may be compared with another homogeneous cluster.

A fourth approach is to measure quality explicitly and relate this information to the output *quantity*. This may happen in two ways. First, a combined measure is developed, mostly using quality as a weight for quantity. This improved quantity measure stands for quantity and quality. Rosen (1984: 37) multiplies output by a quality value K, discounting gross output to real qualitative output. This value K is a producer-determined quality on an ordinal scale (for example from one to four for street cleanliness), but theoretically could be consumer-determined satisfaction rates. Others combine output volume, cost, producer quality standards and consumer satisfaction standards (Fukuhara, 1977: 193–4); Hayes, 1977: 84–5; Ammons, 1984: 8–9). This results in a fictitious discounted output.

A fifth approach is to measure quality and to present it as a separate dimension from quantitative concepts such as volume or efficiency. This allows those who want to combine these different concepts to do it according to their own values, weights and views, and not according to so-called objective experts (Grizzle, 1981).

This (very potted) history of quality measurement exhibits a kind of 'progress' in that quality is added to pure quantitative measures; it no longer just disappears in the quantitative priorities, but is considered *sui generis*. As will become clear as we proceed through the case studies, this process of differentiation of quality measures is continuing. What is more, systems are being developed which will enable providers and service users to measure the rate at which one quality attribute (speed, say) is *traded off* against another (accuracy, friendliness) (Brunel University, 1993). The field of quality measurement is at an exciting stage.

It will not surprise readers to learned that the editors and contributors to this book have as yet failed to find any quality measurement system in use which actually meets all the requirements alluded to above. Indeed such a system could not exist. In the real world most existing quality measurement systems do not even allow for the fact that different stakeholders in a service may select different dimensions or characteristics of that service as being those which make the most important contribution to quality.

PART TWO
CASE STUDIES

Introduction

Christopher Pollitt

In Part One we laid out some of the theoretical, conceptual and methodological issues which help make quality such a profoundly rich and sometimes puzzling topic. We now wish to move quickly to consider the manifestations of these issues in the real world. This will be accomplished by presenting a set of case studies drawn from a wide range of services and countries.

As vehicles for promoting understanding, case studies exhibit both strengths and weaknesses, and we owe the reader a few words of preface and warning. Of course, a group of case studies, however carefully selected, cannot deliver the same assurance of *typicalness* or *comprehensiveness* as a scientifically designed sample or census. They cannot be used to identify statistical trends and may even mislead (because of their vividness) as to what is 'average' or 'normal'. They are less successful than other approaches to knowledge building (for example experiments) as tests of specific hypotheses – though they may have an illuminative function even here. They are not strong as generators of law-like formulations. Yet by way of compensation a good case study can offer a sense of almost 'being there', a richness of detail and a firm grasp of the importance of contextual factors (which are sometimes lost in more 'disembodied' surveys). Well-crafted case study descriptions tend to be more holistic, complex and multi-dimensional, and they can more easily give priority to the perceptions and concerns of the actors who are directly involved. Above all they are accessible and memorable, and do not require the reader previously to have acquired some elaborate technical vocabulary or armoury of techniques.

Given these general characteristics of case studies, what are likely to be the advantages and disadvantages of the particular set offered in the following eight chapters? First, it is important to realize that our cases have been chosen to illustrate relatively *successful* attempts at improving service quality. So this is in no way an 'unbiased sample': on the contrary, it is deliberately biased towards examples of quality improvement activities which have had some useful output, whether in the form of raised standards, improved staff motivation, consumer satisfaction or simply (simply?) the generation of new insights or practices. On the other hand we have *not* sought to collect exclusively cases of the very best or most sophisticated approaches: indeed, some of the techniques used in our cases are fairly straightforward. Our brief to contributing authors was simply that we wanted them to choose cases from which some positive lessons or achievements had come – and that therefore, by implication, they should avoid 'disaster stories' or projects which had produced more bureaucracy and resentment than benefit. Unfortunately cases of the latter type are far from unusual in the world of public service quality improvement.

Secondly, we have attempted to cover a variety of service sectors: universities, an equipment ministry, a military logistics organization, a telecommunications corporation, two local authorities (in different countries), an NHS acute hospital and a police force. We think this variety is important because (as we argue later) the characteristics or circumstances of a service may have important implications for what kind of quality improvement technique will work well and what will not.

Thirdly, the cases vary in terms of scope and level. In Chapter 1 we distinguished between three levels: macro-, meso- and micro-quality. The cases are arranged in a roughly descending order, with the first being a broad-scope study of macro-quality across the entire higher education systems of Western Europe and the later ones focusing on single organizations or parts of single organizations. Chapter 8, for example, deals with micro-quality on one hospital ward.

Fourthly, we draw on the experiences of many different countries. This helps to illustrate the importance of different national administrative cultures in shaping and constraining the quality debate. Although perhaps more explicitly handled in some chapters than in others (Chapter 5 for example), the cultural variable is always worthy of attention, and will be discussed again in more general terms in Part Three of the book.

Each case is intended to stand as an interesting analysis in itself, and some readers may wish to turn directly to a chapter dealing with a service or organization of special interest to them. However, we also wish to explore the extent to which any more general themes can be extracted from the collection of case studies as a whole. This exploration (inevitably tentative given such a variety of cases) is reserved until the final part of the book (Part Three). There we will retrospectively attempt to apply a more general model to the particular instances examined in the case studies. In the last chapter we close the circle by returning to the wider concerns with democratic accountability and participation which we raised in Chapter 1.

3

Quality Measurement and Quality Assurance in European Higher Education

Franz van Vught and Don F. Westerheijden

The increasing focus on quality

In many European countries the concept of quality has become one of the central focuses of attention in the debates on higher education and higher education policy-making. Especially since the early 1980s, quality has been a growing concern in many European higher education systems. In the United Kingdom (in 1984) Sir Keith Joseph declared that the principal objectives for higher education should be 'quality' and 'value for money'. In France in the same year the Comité National d'Évaluation was set up. In the Netherlands in 1985 a governmental policy paper was published called *Higher Education: Autonomy and Quality* (MOW, 1985). In several other countries discussions started about the need to set up a quality assessment system.

Several factors can be indicated that may explain the recent increase in attention to quality in higher education. One important factor lies in the general societal concern about the increase in public expenditure in general. Given this concern, questions are being raised about the priority to be given to higher education within the list of other socially desirable activities. The simple fact that the limits of public expenditure have been reached in many countries, and that budget cuts and retrenchment operations are becoming a familiar litany, leads to questions about the relative quality of the activities that are being financed by public means.

A second factor that may explain the increase in attention to quality is related to the expansion of the Western European higher education systems. The rapid growth of the student body during recent decades, and the accompanying increase in the number of fields of study (especially in the social sciences), departments and even whole new institutions, have intensified societal discussions about the amount and direction of public expenditure for higher education.

A third factor might be the increased 'openness' in many sectors of present-day societies. Not only improved communication facilities, both nationally and internationally, but also the general concern for 'accountability' in various sectors of society, mean that higher education institutions can no long be a 'secret garden' in which the academic oligarchy can hide from the rest of society. Higher education institutions are being challenged to explain to society at large *what* they are doing and *how well* they are doing it.

A fourth factor might be the increased international mobility of students, teachers and researchers in Europe, and the international-ization of the European labour market. These developments have led to a growing need to understand the equivalence of qualifications, standards and credits in the various European higher education systems and thus to more attention being paid to quality assessment systems.

In the *Memorandum on Higher Education in the European Community* (CEC, 1991: 14) this last factor is clearly recognizable:

> The widening perspectives of higher education institutions in Europe would add a European dimension to the entire question of quality. Quality judgements would tend to influence institutional choices in the establishment of partnerships and participation in networks within European structures and would also be a factor in the granting of academic recognition and hence in facilitating mobility. These judge-ments would also come into play among students in exercising their choice of institution and course in a more open and accessible European market for higher education. Employers, too, will need to exercise quality judgements in a single European labour market in which mobility is underpinned by mutual recognition of diplomas for professional pur-poses.

The factors that can explain the recent increase in attention to quality in higher education indicate that what have been called the 'extrinsic values' of higher education have become more important in Western Europe since the early 1980s. The extrinsic values of higher education are related to the services that higher education insti-tutions provide to society. The extrinsic values can be distinguished from the intrinsic qualities of higher education, which are found in the ideals of the search for truth and the pursuit of knowledge (van Vught, 1991).

The expansion of the Western European higher education systems and the increased costs of these systems more and more have to be legitimized by clearly definable societal benefits. Higher education institutions are increasingly confronted with the need to show their relevance, quality and accountability to society. At the same time, the further internationalization of European higher education under-lines the importance of the creation of quality assessment systems that can provide relevant information in a comparative, international context.

Quality as a concept

While it may be clear that attention to the extrinsic values of higher education has grown, this does not imply that quality is a perfectly clear concept in this field. To underline this, it may be pointed out that several recent publications on quality assessment contain the following well-known citation from Robert Pirsig's book *Zen and the Art of Motorcycle Maintenance* (1974):

> Quality . . . you know what it is, yet you don't know what it is. But that's self-contradictory. But some things *are* better than others, that is, they have more quality. But when you try to say what the quality is, apart from the things that have it, it all goes *poof*! There's nothing to talk about. But if you can't say what Quality is, how do you know what it is, or how do you know that it even exists? If no one knows what it is, then for all practical purposes it doesn't exist at all. But for all practical purposes it really *does* exist. What else are the grades based on? Why else would people pay fortunes for some things and throw others in the trash pile? Obviously some things are better than others . . . but what's the 'betterness'? . . . So round and round you go, spinning mental wheels and nowhere finding any place to get traction. What the hell is Quality? What *is* it?

Pirsig's question has been repeated regularly in publications in the field of higher education. According to several authors, quality is a concept which cannot easily be grasped in higher education (Ball, 1985; Williams, 1991). However, it may be pointed out that Pirsig comes close to an *essentialist* view on quality. Characteristic for the essentialist view on quality is the search for an answer to the question: what is the essence of quality? But from an essentialist point of view, quality simply cannot be judged or compared. It should not be surprising that Pirsig's hero went crazy when he thought he had found the essence of quality.

Instead of an essential perspective on quality, a *nominalist* point of view could be taken as the point of departure. The nominalist approach implies an instrumentalist interpretation of the concept of quality, leaving aside the disturbing question of what quality *really* is (Popper, 1957: Section 1.10; Popper, 1983: 262). Quality, in this sense, could be defined as 'fitness for purpose' (Ball, 1985), a defi-nition which indicates a notion that the quality of a phenomenon de-pends upon the subject's view on the purposes of that phenomenon.

This implies that 'there are as many definitions of quality in higher education as there are stakeholders (such as students, teaching staff, scientific communities, government and employers), *times* the number of purposes, or dimensions, these stakeholders distinguish' (Brennan et al., 1992: 13). In this chapter we will take the nominalist position as a point of departure. But we will add to that the view that from the practice of quality management in higher education some common notions can be derived that may be helpful in discussing the concept of quality in higher education. We will come back to these common notions later on.

However, one point already can be emphasized here. Systems of mass higher education require that the higher education institutions in these systems meet a diversity of student needs and abilities, as well as a variety of demands of society. A crucial dimension of higher education quality therefore is to be found in the very diversity of a higher education system.

With respect to the quality of higher education in the United States, Birnbaum (1989) has made a similar point. Birnbaum makes a distinction between three views on quality: the meritocratic, the social and the individualistic views. The meritocratic view refers to quality based on 'institutional conformity to universalistic professional and scholarly norms and uses the academic profession as a reference group'. The social view considers the 'degree to which the institution satisfies the needs of important collective constituents'. The individualistic view emphasizes 'the contribution that the institution makes to the personal growth of students'. Birnbaum formulates the following conclusion (1989: 33):

> When one focuses on institutions, there is a tendency to expect them all to give major attention to meritocratic values. However, given the limited resources available, such expectations inevitably require less attention to other aspects of quality, and thereby diminishes the diversity of the system. It may be argued that the American system of higher education would be weakened significantly if any of these three views of quality disappeared or diminished. It is the tension between the views that provides the diversity that protects and strengthens the higher education system.

Focus of the study

Countries involved

This study is the result of a short project, commissioned by the Liaison Committee of the European Rectors' Conferences and

Table 3.1 *Example of a typology of quality assessment practices*

	1	2	3	4
Aim	Improvement oriented	Accountability oriented		
Scope	Teaching	Research	Service to society	Management
Focus	Input	Process	Output	
Method	Objective ('performance indicators')	Subjective ('peer review')		
Time frame	*Ex ante*	*Ex post*		
Principal	Government	Collective of higher education institutions	Individual higher education institution	External actors
Agent	Government or 'independent' government agencies	Collective of higher education institutions	Individual higher education institution	External actors

sponsored by the European Commission. The objective of the project has been to provide more insight into how quality of higher education is assessed and managed in the various Western European countries. More specifically, the desire was expressed that with the expected further integration of the European Community and its expansion with EFTA countries, a broadly based overview of the mechanisms and procedures for quality management in higher education should be developed, and some indication of a set of common elements of higher education quality management should be given.

For this reason, in the project all 12 member states of the then European Community were selected, as well as the six countries of the European Free Trade Association. With respect to all these countries an effort was made to gather information on the actual, present-day activities regarding higher education quality management.

In principle it would be possible to order the variety of quality management practices in Western Europe using a typology in which a number of relevant concepts are included. An example of such a typology is shown in Table 3.1. Such a typology would, perhaps, provide detailed insight but would be rather cumbersome to use. Therefore, in this project we have collapsed the various dimensions of the typology into two 'ideal types' of combinations that appear to exist in the Western European practices of quality management.

Structure of the chapter
Following on from the preceding discussion, the next two sections will address the 'traditional' and the 'new' methods of quality management in higher education. Since the traditional methods exist in almost all countries and since they are well known, we shall only discuss them briefly here. More attention will be paid to the new methods of quality management which have evolved since the early 1980s in the various Western European higher education systems. In the final section we shall present a synthesis of the findings. In this synthesis the common elements of the new methods will be emphasized.

Limitations in scope
Within the limits of a concise overview of the state of the art of quality assessment in higher education in Western Europe it is not possible to deal with all relevant subjects. We have focused, therefore, on the general systems of quality assessment that have developed or will develop in the future. On this level of information, it is possible to view the experiences in other countries as different possible principles for setting up quality assessment systems in one's own national higher education system. How *exactly* to elaborate such a principle into a working system, fitting into the national political and economic situation, into the national higher education traditions and cultures, and into the national customs of legislation, is a much more complicated matter and cannot be treated in any report of this kind. This is one of the side effects (which can be valued either positively or negatively) of the European richness of national histories and cultures.

By the same token, we shall not go into the matter of how *exactly* quality is assessed or 'measured': that is, what the precise procedures are and which 'performance indicators' – if any – are used. This too depends, in our view, to a large extent on specific national circumstances. And it must be remarked that national circumstances tend to change: as a result, lists of performance indicators, for example tend to change too.

All we can do here is refer the reader to the existing literature on this subject, among others: CVCP (1985; 1987), CVCP/UGC (1987;1989), Cave et al. (1988), Dochy et al. (1990a; 1990b), Findlay (1990), Kells (1990), Johnes and Taylor (1990), Sizer (1990), Yorke (1990) and Sizer et al. (1992). The Journal of the programme on institutional management in higher education (IMHE, part of the OECD), *Higher Education Management*, devoted most of an issue to this topic as recently as 1992: Kells (1992), Spee and Bormans (1992), Sizer (1992), Middaugh and Hollowell (1992), Stolte-Heiskanen (1992), Linke (1992) and Lucier (1992).

Traditional methods of quality management in European higher education

In the literature on higher education, a distinction is usually made between two clusters of traditions of higher education in Europe: the British tradition and the continental tradition (see e.g. Clark, 1983). Since the mode of control, including quality control, in those traditions is one of the distinguishing differences, we think it useful to apply the same distinction here.

The continental tradition

Of old, higher education has been a state-controlled activity in most continental European countries. In both the German (Humboldtian) and the French (Napoleonic) traditions this has been the case, and both traditions have acted as models for many other continental European countries. Hence we shall call these, as did Clark (1983), the *continental traditions*. Of course, large differences exist between the Humboldtian and the Napoleonic traditions, too. An important difference is that in the Humboldtian tradition the *Lehr- und Lernfreiheit* is heavily emphasized, whereas in the Napoleonic tradition state control extends not only over the content of curricula, but also over modes of delivery and student behaviour. Nevertheless, in many respects both continental traditions have had similar influences on the relationships between the state and higher education. In the short characterizations that follow, we shall take the shared continental traditions as a starting point for our discussion.

How did – and does – the continental system of state control over higher education operate in general? Its first and probably most important characteristic is that it operates by way of *ex ante* controls. The overarching, implicit goal is to employ higher education in the country effectively for the good of the government and the national economy. This goal follows from the fact that the government is the largest – often the sole – funder of higher education. The most important mechanisms of traditional continental quality control are, concerning the *input* into higher education:

- *Institution*   Yearly appropriation of the line-item budget.
- *Academic staff*   Civil servant status for the academic staff with

concomitant quality controls (such as diploma requirements or competitive examinations) and special state appointment of full professors. Staff remuneration is government regulated and equal for all institutions of a certain category of higher education.

- *Students*   Competition for student places, for example through entrance exams.

The *process* of education is under *ex ante* control through:

- *Approval*   Procedures of approval of the curriculum of new study programmes or new higher education entities (faculties or whole institutions);
- *Prescription*   Sometimes detailed prescription of the curriculum and the examinations.

Moreover, *ex post* control of the application of the governmentally endorsed prescriptions regarding the educational process is effected, in some cases, through a government inspectorate. Finally, the *output* of higher education (graduates) is controlled, in this ideal type of the continental higher education traditions, through a mixed *ex ante* and *ex post* procedure, namely:

- *Degrees*   *Ex ante* drawing up criteria for, and *ex post* application of additional exams for, national degrees.

These and other forms of governmental control have ensured that the level and quality of higher education in Europe is much more homogeneous than is the case in, for example, the USA – even though the organizational forms of the higher education systems are more heterogeneous. This often takes the form of the assumption that all institutions of a category of higher education are equal as regards their quality; in other words, the existence of a status hierarchy among higher education institutions of their faculties is denied for all governmental purposes.

Such quality control measures are applied in the different European countries to all or some sectors of higher education, depending on historical and political circumstances. Noticeably, some fields of knowledge – or rather, some professions – have been under closer state control, such as medicine, law, engineering and teacher training. Again, the number of fields and the degree of state control vary for the different countries.

The British tradition
In the British tradition state control was much less developed than in the continental model (see e.g. Clark, 1983: 125–9). Relatively more

power and autonomy were given to the higher education institutions through their charters. The British universities, accordingly, were free to develop their own forms of quality control. The universities traditionally were free to select their own staff, according to their own criteria and on their own conditions (including salary levels), and to select their students in the way they wanted (all applying to *input*); to devise their own curriculum (*process*); and to award their own degrees (quality control of *output*). As in continental Europe, until recently the quality of university education was taken for granted.

Even when government funding grew in importance, the distribution of the funds remained in the hands of the academics, through the University Grants Committee (UGC). In more recent years the UGC has been replaced by the University Funding Council (UFC), which is more closely connected with the government.

The most important mechanism for the *collective* upkeep of the academic standards of quality of the *output* have been the external examiners. External examiners are experienced academics with a high reputation in an area of knowledge related to the course to be examined, from other higher education institutions. They report on student work, judging whether it is of comparable quality standards as applied elsewhere.

For a limited number of fields, the system of external examiners was – and still is – complemented by professional licensing or accreditation from interest groups in society (a mechanism which also exists on the continent, though in the latter case this is often supported by governmental control). Accreditation was in place for, among others, engineering and accounting. In those fields, undergraduate degree courses gave exemption from certain professional examinations.

As in many continental countries, teacher training is strictly controlled both regarding numbers of students admitted and the curriculum.

During the 1980s the traditional methods of quality management in European higher education, both in the continental and in the British tradition, have been supplemented by a growing number of new methods. In the next section we shall address these newly developed approaches to higher education quality management.

New methods of quality management in European higher education

Not many countries have a non-traditional system of quality control for higher education in place, although many have plans. Therefore, an exposition of developments in quality control in the countries which do have new methods of operative quality control may have an important function in providing examples (either positive or negative) to decision-makers in other higher education systems. In this section, accordingly, we shall concentrate on the higher education systems where new methods of quality control have been developed and put into practice before 1992, especially those in France, the Netherlands and the United Kingdom.

It should be pointed out that in this section we shall not explore the differences in the development of the quality management systems of the university and the non-university sectors in detail. Such an exploration would certainly be interesting and lessons can probably be learned from it. However, given the framework of the present study this exploration cannot be undertaken.

Another remark concerns a common aspect of the new methods of quality assessment in the countries mentioned, which is difficult to point out in the mechanisms themselves. This is the general aim of these methods of not only providing a manner of state control (or social accountability), but also being directed especially towards quality *improvement* in higher education. The relative weight of the two goals of improvement and accountability differs in the practices of different countries, but in each case the explicit attention to quality improvement of education even at the highest level is an important new development.

Preliminary remarks: quality control, quality assessment
and quality management
Since the exact meaning of the terms 'quality control', 'quality assessment' and 'quality management' is partly dependent on national traditions, we shall give our definitions of these terms first. *Quality control* is defined in technical environments as: 'the operational techniques and activities that are used to fulfil the requirements for quality' (ISO 8402). In this report, it is also used to denote the way of operation concerning quality in higher education in the state control strategy (van Vught, 1989), as characterized earlier. Such traditional quality control does not show an explicit emphasis on quality improvement, as the new methods do, but is explicitly concerned with application to existing (bureaucratic) standards.

Quality management is defined as: 'that aspect of the overall management function that determines and implements the quality policy [intentions and direction of the organization]'. Quality assurance is: 'all those planned and systematic actions necessary to provide *adequate confidence'*. This usage is in accordance with ISO 8402 (emphasis added). Quality assessment is not defined there, but quality audit is. Parallel to quality audit, the term *quality assessment* (which is more common in the field of higher education) will be taken to mean: a systematic examination to determine whether quality activities comply with planned arrangements and whether the 'product' (the educational process) is implemented effectively and is suitable for achieving objectives.

It should be noted, however, that not too much importance should be paid to definitions: in several circumstances it may even be possible to use especially 'quality control' and 'quality management' as synonyms.

France: the Comité National d'Évaluation
The President of the French Republic and an act of parliament brought into being the Comité National d'Évaluation (CNÉ) in 1985 as a result of the so-called *Loi Savary*. It was, accordingly, set up in a spirit of concern about the dysfunctions of the traditional, central-ized, system of quality control: lack of actual autonomy, uniformity, rigidity, bureaucracy and so on (Staropoli, 1991: 45). Given its position in terms of constitutional law, the CNÉ is a government agency, but it only reports to the President, so it is independent of the Prime Minister, the Minister of Education and other executive agencies. The CNÉ is the first of a new type of administrative authority. Its position is, for the same reason, also independent of the higher education institutions it assesses. This intermediate position between the state and the higher education institutions has the advantage that the CNÉ can work independently, hence 'objec-tively'. The disadvantage of such a position is that the committee lacks assured support; in particular, in some circumstances such a position may lead to difficulties in convincing higher education institutions to co-operate in assessments.

The 70 members of the CNÉ are appointed for four years by the President of the Republic (Cazenave, 1990). Eleven members represent the academic community, shortlisted through university and research umbrella organizations. The other six members rep-resent high government agencies: the Conseil Économique et Social (the council of government employers and trade unions), the Conseil d'État (the constitutional court) and the Cour des Comptes (the government accounting office).

The CNÉ quality assessment procedure consists of two parts, institution-wide evaluations and 'horizontal', disciplinary reviews.

The evaluations are not specific down to the individual level, nor do they assess courses: these two levels are covered by the traditional mechanisms. Where necessary and possible, the CNÉ makes use of existing evaluations and control reports of other agencies that do examine these and other aspects (such as the CNRS research laboratories). The tasks of the CNÉ are concerned not only with quality control (investigating whether higher education institutions produce sufficient quality), but also with judging, quite generally, the results of the contracts established between higher education institutions and the Ministry of Education.[1] Evaluation results are not used directly for making reallocations of funds; however, through the contract negotiations and the annual budget negotiations, a firm link with decision-making is established.

The CNÉ makes institution-wide evaluations of education, research and management, the argument being that research and teaching are interdependent primary activities of higher education institutions. Also, other aspects of the higher education institution as an environment for teaching and research are examined. Evaluations are undertaken after an invitation by the higher education institution; it is a voluntary procedure, though the CNÉ has the right to undertake the evaluations it wants. The CNÉ 'tours' all institutions every eight years approximately, which means that the first round has been complete at the time of writing this report (1992). Each audit results in a report on the institution, making recommendations to the persons responsible for institutional management. These reports are public. They are sent, among others, to the ministers responsible for the higher education institutions visited, so as to assure the reports' roles in the negotiations mentioned above. The whole procedure, from invitation to report, takes about one year (see also Neave, 1991).

The second part of the CNÉ procedure consists, first, of self-evaluation reports provided by the institution to be visited. These reports are confidential (and include names on individuals). Secondly, the CNÉ, the institution involved and government offices collect statistical data (not necessarily performance indicators). With those two sources and its own visit to the location, an external peer committee makes qualitative judgements, resulting in a public report. The committees consist of about 15–20 persons, of which most are academics, but about 10 per cent come from industry and about 5 per cent are foreigners. These committees work 'horizontally', reviewing all courses in a broad disciplinary area.

Every year, the CNÉ presents a summary report to the President.

In the reports the CNÉ gives an overview of its institution-wide evaluations. However, no explicit rankings are made of the institutions audited. The character of the reports is sometimes judged to be descriptive rather than analytical (Guin, 1990).

The Netherlands: quality assessment co-ordinated by the umbrella organizations

Following the publication of the policy paper entitled *Higher Education: Autonomy and Quality* (MOW, 1985), the relationships between the Ministry of Education and science and the higher education institutions in the Netherlands were restructured. In exchange for a greater degree of financial and managerial autonomy, the higher education institutions would prove to society (in fact, to the government) that they delivered quality education. (A quality assessment system for research had already been operational since the beginning of the 1980s.) Originally, the government intended this evaluation to be executed by the Inspectorate for Higher Education (IHO), in part newly established. In subsequent discussions the umbrella organizations of the higher education institutions, the Association of Co-operating Universities in the Netherlands (VSNU) for the universities and the HBO Council for non-university higher education institutions, took that responsibility on themselves. The IHO was bypassed through that compromise and was largely left with the task of 'meta-evaluation': evaluation of the evaluation. A pilot project was held by the VSNU in 1988. As a consequence of the evaluation of the pilot project (VSNU, 1988) some adjustments were made and the quality assessment procedure became operational in 1989. In 1990 the HBO Council started a procedure in the non-university sector that, although not completely similar to the VSNU approach, is based on the same principles. For reasons of brevity we shall concentrate on the VSNU system. This system is 'owned' (and funded) by the universities collectively. This has led to a change in emphasis as regards the aims of quality assessment: from a predominant emphasis on accountability a shift has taken place to a primary emphasis on quality improvement. In other words, in practice, goals requiring formative quality judgements have come to the fore at the expense of goals requiring summative quality judgements.

The procedure is summarized in Figure 3.1. The focal point of the VSNU quality assessment procedure is the visiting committee that reviews all study programmes in a given area of knowledge in the country (until now a maximum of nine study programmes in the 13 universities). In preparation for the visiting committee, each

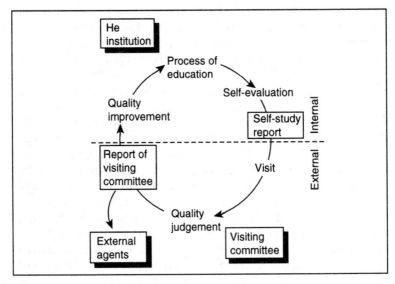

Figure 3.1   *The cycle of quality assessment in Dutch universities*

participating study programme is required to write a self-evaluation. As the aims of the self-evaluation are not only the preparation of the faculty for the visiting committee, but also the stimulation of internal quality management (Vroeijenstijn and Acherman, 1990: 88), the content of the self-evaluation is not fixed completely: the faculties and departments to be evaluated can stress points which are important to them. However, for reasons of comparability, a fixed format is given by the VSNU checklist (VSNU, 1990).

The checklist consists of a large number of subjects that should be addressed in the self-evaluation; it is not a list of performance indicators, either quantitative or qualitative, though some data might be interpreted in that way (such as student completion rates). The self-studies of all participating study programmes are collected by the visiting committee before it starts on its 'tour' of the country.

The visiting committees consist of about seven members, including at least one foreign expert of the field (with knowledge of the Dutch language and the Dutch higher education situation) and one educational expert. The other members are preferably chosen from other parts of Dutch higher education than the participating pro-grammes and from the professional field; an even distribution over the several sub-specialisms is aimed for. In practice, special care is taken to appoint an independent chair. Experimentally, in one visiting committee a student representative has been appointed in 1991–2. The members of the committee are proposed by the collective of representatives of the participating faculties and nominated by the board of the VSNU. The committee visits each study programme for two or two and a half days. During this period the committee speaks with representatives of all interest groups in the faculty, including students. To enable non-selected voices to be heard, an 'open hour' is part of the procedure. Subjects for the talks are taken from the self-evaluation, from the committee's prior visits and other (usually considerable) knowledge of the field and the faculty, and whatever else comes up during the visit. At the end of the visit, the chair gives an oral, provisional judgement about the quality of the study programme. Based on the written version of this judgement and the (factual) comments of the study programmes, the visiting committee then writes its final report. The report usually contains a general part, stating problems, outlooks, expectations and recommendations pertaining to all of the field, and chapters about the individual study programmes.

The recommendations in the visiting committee report supposedly lead to improvements in the study programmes, together with the measures taken based on the self-evaluations in anticipation of the visiting committee. The initial results of research into the institutional follow-up indicate that this does indeed happen to a certain extent, though not in a clear, linear fashion. Nor have the measures taken up to now been very drastic (Westerheijden et al., 1992). As shown in Figure 3.1, the visiting committee report is also read by external agents. For example, the IHO writes a yearly report about the visiting committees, its 'meta-evaluation' report. Coverage in the newspapers is also usual.

As a result of the agreements of 1986, the Ministry of Education and Science has not taken any action on the basis of the visiting committee's judgements. It was thought that the introduction of the system should not be hampered by direct consequences for decision-making and funding. Direct links to funding and other aspects of government decision-making would lead only too easily to strategic behaviour on the part of the higher education institutions which would undermine the quality assessment system completely. A way has been found, however, to escape from what may be called (Westerheijden, 1990: 206) the *dilemma of quality assessment*:

> Without the expectation of real consequences, the incentives to organize quality assessment are lacking; with the expectation of real consequences, quality assessment will turn into a power game.

The Ministry of Education and Science has found its way out, as said before, by abstaining from direct intervention, but simultaneously making it known that it *may* take action in the medium or long term.

The United Kingdom: two models

In the United Kingdom, two models of quality management have been developed since the enlargement of government influence over higher education in the 1960s. The first model applies to the sector of non-university higher education, the polytechnics and colleges. Much later, quality control was extended to university higher education too. We shall characterize these models in their chronological order. It should be noted that owing to the changes in the higher education system as a result of the White Paper *Higher Education: a New Framework* (DES, 1991), formalized in the Further and Higher Education Act of 1992, new arrangements are beginning to take shape at the time of writing this report.

The first model is that of validation and accreditation by the Council for National Academic Awards (CNAA). Since the first half of the 1960s non-university higher education in the UK has been under the aegis of the CNAA (Brennan, 1990). As in other countries, quality in this higher education sector was also controlled by Her Majesty's Inspectorate (HMI), which continued to exist, with its own responsibilities and methods, alongside the new CNAA. HMI judgements fed into, among others, funding decisions by the Polytechnics and Colleges Funding Council (PCFC). The main characterizing element of HMI procedures was classroom observation.

The CNAA, a government-initiated body, was independent: it obtained its own royal charter in 1964. It was a degree-awarding body, giving out degrees of a professedly equal level to those of universities (bachelor's degree). The CNAA validated proposed courses in colleges and polytechnics *ex ante* and reviewed them quinquennially. For a long time the committees consisted of peers, that is academics working in the same area of knowledge, but in other higher education institutions (colleges, polytechnics *and* universities), plus, if applicable, representatives of the relevant profession or industry. These committees based their visit on detailed written information regarding the structure and content of the course, ways and methods of teaching and student assessment, and available resources (research and teaching qualifications of the staff members who were expected to become involved, physical equipment and so on). In the frequent cases of disapproval by the committee a new round, based on an amended proposal, would start. The periodic reviews were similar, though as a rule less uncertain as regards the committee's approval. Moreover, the CNAA had to approve the appointment of external examiners for the public sector institutions.

The peer review of courses was complemented by a review, usually quinquennial, of the institution's own operational (that is, not just existing on paper) mechanisms to assure the level of its courses. Later, since 1988, the CNAA *accredited* a number of polytechnics to validate their own courses (undergraduate and postgraduate degree level) through monitoring of the institutional quality management procedures. These procedures included annual internal monitoring systems and public performance indicators.

Based on this tradition of government-independent quality assessment, the CNAA and the PCFC tried to liberalize the evaluation culture developing in the 1980s, which was becoming more and more 'continental' in its government-centred approach, by taking account of the institution's goals and aims (Kogan, 1991). With the end of the binary line in 1992, the CNAA ceased to exist at the beginning of that year.

The second model is that of quality audit by the Academic Audit Unit (AAU). The turning points in quality management for British universities were two reports in the mid 1980s: the Reynolds Report to the University Grants Committee (UGC) and the Jarratt Report to the Committee of Vice-Chancellors and Principals (CVCP). In the Reynolds Report criteria were laid down for internal quality management systems which all universities would be required to introduce in the following years. The Jarratt Report was the focal point for the discussion of performance indicators and their role in quality-based funding.

The AAU was introduced in 1990–1 by the umbrella organization of the universities, the CVCP, reputedly to counter the threat of HMI to extend its control to the universities as well (Kogan, 1991: Young, 1990). Before, as explained in the section on the UK tradition, each university individually took care of its quality control. The external, comparative aspect in this system consisted of the external examiners. Views differ on the effectiveness of these external examiners in terms of quality assessment. However, this approach was judged to be an insufficient mechanism for providing accountability towards society in general and to the government in particular. The AAU had to fill this gap.

The background of the AAU's methods is threefold: CNAA procedures, financial audits and total quality management. The

CNAA has been discussed in the previous section. Financial external audits provide a check for the outside world that the organization's bookkeeping systems are in order and look at some examples to see how they operate. Likewise, the AAU quality audit checks whether the university's quality management systems are sufficient and, through 'tracing' some examples, how they really operate. AAU activities are, therefore, a form on 'meta-evaluation': the AAU evaluates not the quality of higher education, but the quality of the institution's evaluation methods. From the total quality management (TQM) movement the AAU borrows among others the ideas of the crucial role of customer (students and employers) satisfaction, staff training and development for quality, and the idea that the quality of higher education is dependent on the totality of an institution's activities.

The core of the AAU quality assessment procedure consists of an on-site visit by an audit team. The teams consist of academics, as a rule two or three persons. The choice of institutions to visit results from 'negotiated invitation'. In preparation for its (usually three-day) visit the audit team receives written information from the university on the quality assessment systems it has, plus – if requested – a small number of examples of the application of these systems. The AAU has a checklist based on good practice against which to assess an institution's quality assessment mechanisms. The checklist includes topics like curriculum data (organization and planning processes), teaching method, staff quality data, reports or opinions from external examiners and from students, and so on. From this documentation together with the information gathered during the on-site visit the audit team drafts a short report for the university as a whole and, if necessary, confidential reports on 'sensitive issues' to the vice-chancellor. Following the institution's comments on this draft a final version is written of the official report. The AAU does not itself publish the report, but the university is encouraged to do so.

Towards a European dimension in higher education quality management?

In this study it has become clear that in many Western European countries new procedures and mechanisms for quality management are being developed. In many countries discussions about these new approaches are still ongoing. In some countries new quality management systems appear to be in operation. The first experiences with these systems have been presented in the previous section. In this section we shall concentrate on a general comparative exploration of the quality management systems in operation in Western Europe. In particular we shall present an inventory of the common elements of these systems.

Surveying the experiences with the new quality management system in several Western European countries, it can be argued that in these systems a number of similar elements are to be found. The various national quality management systems that either have been recently introduced or are still in a process of development of course all have their own specific characteristics. It may be expected that these national idiosyncrasies will continue to exist in the future. But the systems that are already in operation also show some similar elements, which offer us as opportunity to present an overview of the common elements in the systems of quality management in Western Europe. The common elements to a large extent are deduced from the similarities in the quality management systems of especially France, the Netherlands and the United Kingdom. It is in these countries that the new methods and procedures of quality management so far have been implemented most widely. It is from the experiences in these countries that we can learn about the positive and negative effects of the new quality management systems.

Common elements of the new methods of quality management in European higher education

We should emphasize beforehand that the common elements to be presented here certainly do not encompass all aspects of quality management in higher education. Most importantly, the scope of the presentation is on teaching, not on research or institutional management. The focus is on the process. And the aims behind the elements are both institutional quality improvement and accountability towards society. This does not imply other aspects are unimportant in our opinion. What it does imply is that we regard the elements presented here to have priority, particularly in the light of the experience building up in the European countries at present.

The experiences with quality management in especially the United Kingdom, the Netherlands and France seem to lead towards a set of common elements of quality management. Recent approaches used by the CNAA and the CVCP's Academic Audit Unit in the United Kingdom, by the Association of Co-operating Universities in the Netherlands and by the French Comité National d'Évaluation appear to be rather similar. What then are these common elements?

A first element has to do with the managing agent or (agents) of the quality management system. Such an agent should be independent and have the responsibility to manage the system at the meta level. The *meta-level agent* should be the co-ordinator of the quality management system, acting independently from government and not having the task to impose upon the institutions an approach that the government deems to be necessary. The meta-level agent should preferably have some legal basis. Its co-ordinating task should imply (after consultation with the institutions) the formulation of procedures and formats that can be used by the institutions. In these procedures and formats consistent statistical information can be indicated as highly relevant. The experiences in the various countries in Western Europe show that exactly this meta-level role is of great importance to obtain acceptance of the system. The AAU in the United Kingdom neither inspects courses and programmes, nor validates courses. The AAU only monitors and comments on the mechanisms by which the institutions themselves assure the quality of the programmes they offer (Williams, 1991). Similarly, in the procedures used by the CNAA since 1985, the institutions were encouraged to undertake their own quality review processes. While the CNAA kept its responsibility for the final approval of the courses leading to its awards, the quality management mechanism first of all had to do with the institution's capacity to identify its strengths and weaknesses and to improve its quality. The VSNU in the Netherlands follows a similar strategy. In the quality management system in the Netherlands the emphasis is put on the institution's self-evaluation and the visit by peers. The VSNU itself only operates as the co-ordinator of the system.

A second common element in the new quality management systems is the mechanism of *self-evaluation* (or self-study, self-assessment). It is often argued in the higher education literature that, in order for academics to accept and implement changes, they must trust and 'own' the process in which problems are defined and solutions are designed. This is certainly also the case in quality management. Only if the academics accept quality management as their own activity will the system be successful. Self-evaluation is a crucial mechanism for academics to accept a quality management system. Moreover, in a self-evaluation process (or in any set of activities in a higher education institution with a focus on internal quality assessment), consultation with outside actors (employers, alumni) is of great importance. Also, it may be pointed out that the self-evaluation activities should be guided by the general procedures and formats that were discussed with the meta-level agent. The

evaluation of the first pilot year of the experiences in the Netherlands with the new management system (in which self-evaluation
plays a crucial role) confirms this insight. The faculties (departments) that undertook a self-evaluation indicate that they felt their
self-studies to be relevant and useful. They especially indicated that
the self-studies appear to be important incentives for adapting
existing programmes and routines (Vroeijenstijn and Acherman,
1990). Although less elaborated, in the French and the British
systems the idea of self-evaluation also seems to be important. The
CNÉ had indicated that it assumes that information on and from a
higher education institution is available when an evaluation is
carried out. The AAU advises the institutions to produce several
'briefing documents', the purpose of which is to ensure that the
auditing team forms a clear view of the quality assurance systems in
operation.

A third common element in the new quality management systems
certainly appears to be the mechanism of *peer review* and especially
one or more *site visits* by external experts. It is crucial that these
external experts should be accepted by the institution to be visited
as unbiased specialists in the field. They can come from many
constituencies (including employers' organizations, industry and
professional bodies) and, depending on the nature of the visit
(review of a specific study programme or management audit at the
institutional level), they will need to have specific backgrounds
(academic expertise, managerial experience and so on). The external visitors should visit the institution (or faculty/department) for a
period of a few days, during which they can discuss the self-
evaluation report and the plans for future innovations with the
faculty. The visitors could also take the opportunity to interview
staff, students, administrators and (if possible) alumni. This
element appears to be used successfully in several Western European quality management systems. In the UK the CNAA has
always emphasized the visit by a committee of peers. The AAU sees
the visit as an intense and concentrated activity (Williams,
1991: 7–8):

> During three days the audit team will talk to probably more than hundred
> people in some twenty or so sessions, ranging from the Vice-Chancellor to
> first-year students. Each session will have a different purpose, but all will
> be informed by the team's need not only to satisfy itself that it understands
> what is supposed to happen, and the extent to which is actually does so,
> but also the extent to which the mechanisms and structures in place are
> adequate and appropriate to meet the quality assurance needs of the
> institution in terms of its own stated aims and objectives.

In France the CNÉ organizes at least two visits to each university being reviewed. In the Netherlands a team of external experts visits each programme site of a specific discipline. By doing so the peer review process takes the form of a comparative analysis, although the purpose certainly does not include ranking the individual programme sites. The idea behind the comparative analysis is to help the external visitors to get a good impression of the state of the art in the discipline. A crucial aspect to be emphasized in a quality management system with a European dimension is the inclusion in the review committees of international experts. They in particular can pay attention to the European aspects of programmes and institutions.

A fourth element in the new methods of quality management in European higher education concerns the *reporting* of the results of and experience with these methods. Regarding this element, it may first of all be pointed out that some form of reporting the conclusions of the peer review team is very useful. However, such a report should not have the function of judging or ranking the institutions or programmes that have been visited. It rather should have as its main objective to help the institutions and study programmes to improve their levels of quality. A crucial phase in the reporting process therefore concerns providing the opportunity to the institutions and units that have been visited to comment on a draft version of the report and to formulate counter-arguments if necessary. Also, in the final version of the report higher education institutions should be able to indicate possible disagreements with the peer review team. Reporting the results of the quality assessment processes is an important mechanism in the process of providing accountability to external constituencies. However, there appear to be various ways of offering such a report and each has its specific advantages and disadvantages. One way is to publish the complete report and, by so doing, to offer it to all those who might be interested. The advantage of such an approach is that each constituency can immediately and clearly find out what the outcomes of an assessment have been and how these outcomes relate to their norms and criteria. A disadvantage of this approach is that it may severely limit the commitment of those who are visited to engage in open discussions with the peer review team, simply because they fear the effects of their frankness when the results of the review are published. A second way to report on the results of the peer review is to offer the detailed report only to the institutions visited and to guarantee confidentiality. To the external constituencies (and to society at large) a general summary of the report can be presented, which may be used as a mechanism for providing accountability. The advantage of this approach is that the commitment of those who are visited will be high. The disadvantage is that some external constituencies might not be satisfied with only a summary of the report, out of fear that information is being withheld from them.

Regarding this element of quality management, the approaches in the various countries differ. In the Netherlands, although in the pilot phase the reports of the external visitors were kept confidential, since the system has been implemented the final overall reports have been made public. The argument for doing so is the accountability objective. The negative effects, which are already becoming visible, are that the reports become rather general and that academics who have been visited pay less attention to the outcomes of the visits (Westerheijden et al., 1992). The French CNÉ also publishes its reports on the institutions. The institutional self-evaluations are kept confidential, while the report by the external experts is public. In the procedures of the British AAU the audit report is intended to provide an accurate account of an institution's quality assurance mechanisms. The report thereby draws attention to good and bad practice. The report is first of all written for the institution and the AAU itself does not publish the reports. It is for the institution to decide what publicity to give to its reports, although it is assumed that the report 'finds its way into the public domain accompanied by a commentary prepared by the University' (Williams, 1991: 10).

A final common element of the new approaches to quality management concerns the possible relationship between the outcomes of a quality review and the (governmental) decisions about the funding of higher education activities. Based on the experience of quality management in Western Europe so far, we can argue that a *direct, rigid relationship* between quality review reports and funding decisions should *not* be established. By a direct, rigid relationship we mean that the quality judgements are the only input into the funding process, and moreover that a simple linear function is applied: good education means so much extra money, and bad education so much less money. Such an 'automatic' direct relationship will probably harm the operation of a quality management system – all the more so as funding decisions at present tend to be cutbacks (negative sanctions) rather than incentives (positive sanctions). With such a rigid relationship academics and institutions will distrust the external review teams and they will produce self-evaluation studies in compliance with perceived criteria but with little real interest. Relating a system of rigid and direct rewards and sanctions to the delicate mechanism of quality management may have a very negative effect on the operation of the system (Westerheijden, 1990).

In France, the CNÉ has understood these dangers. Its evaluations do not have a direct impact on state subventions to the institutions. The new plans with respect to quality management in the United Kingdom do imply creating a direct relationship between quality management and funding. The danger of this is that it may lead to a compliance culture, the only aim of which will be to appear to meet the criteria that will be formulated by the new 'assessment units', irrespective of whether those criteria are appropriate in the context of specific institutions or not.

The above does *not* imply that an *indirect*, non-automatic relationship between quality management and funding decisions should also be rejected. On the contrary, as for instance the new approaches in France show, such an indirect relationship, where quality judgements are one – but not the only one – of the inputs into the policy processes leading to funding decisions, could very well be part of the set of common elements presented here.

An indirect relationship would imply that the various national governments (which, in Western European higher education, are the central funding organizations) will only provide the necessary financial means to higher education institutions if these institutions (and the various units within these institutions) can show that they have submitted themselves to at least one external judgement which is an accepted part of the general quality management system. Only if higher education institutions can show that they have offered their educational programmes for external review should these institutions be eligible for government funding. Whether the funds provided by government are used to reward programmes that have been judged to be of good quality, or to help programmes that have received a negative qualification by an external review team, should be the decision of the higher education institution itself. It should be left to the discretion of the higher education institutions how they react to the outcomes of the quality management system. The decision to fund or not to fund an institution (or certain programmes within an institution) should, in this approach, only depend upon the willingness to submit the institutional activities to outside review.

The common elements presented in this section – touching upon the meta-level role of managing agent(s), upon self-evaluation, upon peer review and its visits, upon the degree of confidentiality of reporting, and upon the relationship between quality review outcomes and funding – together form the core of what could be distilled from the new methods of quality management in European higher education. As has been stated above, several options are possible for each of these core elements. These are elements that should be explored further when the experiences with and effects of higher education quality management are being discussed on a European scale. It may also be in these elements that the European dimension of higher education quality management can be found.

Note

1 The four-year contracts between the higher education institution and the Ministry of Education cover, in principle, all activities carried out by the institutions: education, research and so on. The contracts are concerted development programmes, allowing the institutions to emphasize certain objectives in their development more than others.

4

Quality in the French Public Service

Sylvie Trosa

This case study is the result of a survey by the author of the implementation of quality indicators in the French public services. This survey was carried out by a group of experts under the authority of the Scientific Council for Evaluation in France on the request of the Minister of Public Affairs and Administrative Reforms. The group's report was delivered on 4 January 1993.

A history of quality in France

The French public service began its involvement in defining quality in 1980–5. Some services chose quality circles and total quality frameworks. These initiatives remained marginal. Government did not take the opportunity to create a momentum for the whole administration. Today, these initiatives are considered to be failures. Several reasons contributed to their disappointment.

The appropriate organization level for effective initiatives was not very well chosen. Effective quality circles have to be located in coherent, autonomous small organizational structures with certain degrees of freedom. In larger organizations these quality circles tend to trigger a series of complex organizational problems. In other words, QCs functioned well in situations where answers to problems were easily implemented, and failed where answers were drowned in the complexity of hierarchical chains of command and decision.

There was little anticipation by administrative directorates of the consequences of these initiatives in the quality process. It would be an exaggeration to assert that all quality work inflates resource requirements and implies additional means. Yet, it is clear that focusing on dysfunctions may put the need for new investments and the reforms of working procedures into perspective. At that moment, managers have to respond, given the financial degrees of freedom that are available and the timing of the change. Only rarely were these thought of beforehand, so that there were cases of disappointed QCs which did not receive supportive answers to their questions.

Finally, these initiatives were too much oriented towards themselves, exclusively towards internal working procedures, and were not client oriented. Perhaps this can be explained by the fact that total quality management in the French public sector was copying the private sector TQM without taking different system features into account. In the private sector it is acceptable to focus on working procedures and internal standards to the extent that the external market is the guarantee of efficiency. In the absence of a market, which is usually the case in the public sector, a quality definition may totally mismatch user expectations. For example road quality, as seen by an engineer civil servant, that is in terms of technical perfection, may be very distant from driver expectations. Drivers may be willing to accept a lower level of perfection in exchange for a better set of signs and directions.

The present intention is to learn lessons from past problems. There is no unique model that will be imposed or advised. Every administration will have to explore its own implementation plan. The only points insisted upon by government are:

1 No quality steps may be taken without a formal exploration of user expectations.
2 Quality has to measured by indicators which will register changes and evolution.

This case study used two major examples, the Ministry of Equipment and France-Télécom. These two institutions have a long-standing experience in the quality field and represent contrasting steps, methods, and goals.

The case of the Ministry of Equipment: quality as an aid to decision-making

The concept of quality in play was guided by two considerations:

1 The will to motivate workers: quality improvement covers a set of techniques and tools, ranging from group work to methods for problems solving and to value analysis.
2 A concern to respond to demands from clients (which became extremely strong as a consequence of decentralization). Indeed, Departmental Directorates of Equipment (DDEs) continue to work for local communities which contribute a non-negligible part of their finance. These communities wanted to know how their money was spent and what type of service they could expect. The

definition of service quality was in this case an almost inevitable consequence of real decentralization.

The history of the relationship between DDEs and local communities developed through three main steps. First, DDEs analysed the major financial outlays by field of activity (roads, social housing, land and city planning, building regulations and protection of the environment) and by client (state, department, municipality) in order to have a comprehensive picture of the use and allocation of resources. This had a calming influence and showed that none of the partners were delivering more than they were receiving (except for the central state). However, this still did not permit an overview of the nature of the service, or of its quality.

Secondly, to cope with this problem, DDEs started surveys to discover the opinions of their clients, that is the elected officials (strong and very well-organized mayors, in France mostly senators). These surveys resulted in little information, because they asked the elected representatives what they thought of the agencies and their products. This question was usually answered favourably because of the relatively deferential culture. Even when there was a negative appreciation, it was hard for practical alternatives to be formulated, because of a lack of improvement proposals. User groups were put in place. But for such a group to be able to work effectively, there is a need to learn how to work together and to have cases to discuss (not general questions like 'what do you think of this action or this product?'). These preconditions were seldom fulfilled and interesting experiences were abandoned before they could take off.

DDEs then focused on a third way: that of seeking the opinion of the direct users, the non-institutional clients, starting with service-oriented statements on different levels of service delivery (such as 'If you want the streets to be cleared of snow it costs this and implies that', 'If you want it twice' and so on). Elaborating different levels of service delivery implies several requirements:

1 an analysis of tasks and present work schemes to know what and how public servants may perform;
2 drawing out information from the knowledge of providers of clients, especially from those in direct contact with those clients;
3 diagnosis of what resources are available and of costs per activity.

The definition of different levels of service delivery depends upon a monitoring system that will enable answers to be formulated to the following questions. First, what are the specific expectations of clients? Second, what are the specific problems in organizing work? Third, what resources are available? This is therefore a local and service-oriented analysis but one which is strongly integrated in the strategic service monitoring system.

This type of discussion on the level of service can give the impression that the civil service is taking over because civil servants are making the propositions to the clients. In reality it is always the public service which is trading off different aspects or types of services delivered. The procedure is intended to put into place *recurrent* dialogues. It is about confronting user expectations and producer knowledge.

The example of the DDEs shows that quality is neither additional to performance, nor antithetical to productivity. On the contrary, quality is an indispensable extension of performance measures from the point of view of management, as well as for higher-level, supervisory civil servants. It forces management to refine, since it is no longer sufficient simply to measure major financial volumes (such an amount for town planning, but what kind of town planning; such an amount for roads, but what kind of roads). There is pressure to define precisely the services delivered to clients. It puts civil servants into a position to propose scenarios and levels of public intervention. Indeed, at the DDEs management and civil servants were soon asking for definitions of levels of service delivery. In the past, the Ministry asked for analytic accounts, and for the kind of objectives/resources planning which is necessary for the division of inputs. This is almost useless for the relationship with the clients of basic services, because clients want to know the quality and not just the cost of services.

Some of the findings of this case study are therefore as follows:

1 Indicators of quality and other dimensions of performance cannot and should not be aggregated.
2 Indicators are used by supervising civil servants and by management. Information is only delivered to central services if it is useful to explain modernization; there is no obligation to provide this information to the centre.
3 Civil servant involvement in quality steps is valued by the top. All innovation in the field of quality can be made public, distributed and registered (patented); the Ministry is organizing a yearly forum for innovation.

The France-Télécom case: quality as accountability to clients

The quality indicators developed by France-Télécom respond to issues that are very simple but sensitive for the users: delay in repairs;

delay in answering calls; numbers of complaints. Technical indicators, allowing the evaluation of technological network quality, are linked to indicators on the functioning of the organization. One could say that there is a balance between indicators of external goals and indicators responding to the professional concerns of civil servants. These indicators rely on technical measures, or on studies carried out by external organizations, independent from France-Télécom, such as for monitoring user satisfaction. Additionally, all results are forwarded to the board. Every quality measure corresponds to a file of specifications explaining what is measured, why, at what intervals, with what resources, and who is responsible.

Quality at France-Télécom absorbs a significant investment: every indicator is tracked by a responsible person who is controlling a network of correspondents and who is monitoring the data input. Finally, a unit, at the highest level, was created to be able to debate divergent interpretations of indicators. The board of France-Télécom includes delegates from the users, but the unit in charge of the monitoring is an in-house unit, mainly consisting of engineers. In the Télécom case customers are involved in determining and evaluating measures through the board. For example, the delegates of the customers have been able to oblige France-Télécom to send detailed bills to all clients who asked for them, whereas the in-house engineers did not want this. Yet, the weight of the technical experts in this old technical fortress remains enormous.

The management of France-Télécom uses indicators in two ways: as a report to the board; and as an instrument of internal control. The results permit an analysis of the evolution of activities over time (overviews are monthly), and a comparison of several services. Every part of the organization knows the results of the others, as well as its own, Transparency is almost 100 per cent.

At first, the information resulting from the indicators did not significantly affect the allocation of resources. However, there is a possibility of varying the premiums for profitability within the margins of 5–10 per cent of the premium. Recently, an agreement was signed with four major trade unions on a collective interest premium. This would come into effect if quality targets are reached, as determined in the contract between the management and the administration.

This case is, to some extent, the opposite of the preceding DDEs case, because here quality indicators were centrally developed. Two reasons for this were the nature of the products and the objectives set for the indicators. In the case of France-Télécom, products delivered may be directly compared with private sector equivalents. Beyond that, indicators are meant to support accountability to the board and after being made public, to the users. At the DDEs, indicators were developed to help control the work of civil servants, and to adapt more easily to the specific needs of the local communities. In the DDEs case, a major condition for success is that civil servants should develop these measures themselves, and not have them imposed from above. The methods of developing indicators and the degree of participation of civil servants depend upon the objectives set for these indicators; that is, upon whether the development of internal control instruments or of tools to support accountability to users is the priority.

Finally, the base for the indicators is different in the two cases. At France-Télécom indicators result from an analysis, based upon either client expectations or technical expertise. At the DDEs, indicators result from a confrontation between the analysis of the local client communities and a diagnosis of the problems of the functioning of the organization. In both organizations there is an analysis of demand, but in the Télécom case the focus is on global expectations *vis-à-vis* the institution, and not the client-specific desires in a particular context. The difference is partly explained by the fact that France-Télécom is following a functional ratio and the DDEs a territorial ratio.

Common lessons from the two cases

In comparing the DDEs and France-Télécom cases, there are two kinds of lessons: those relating to the methodology for implementing quality improvements and those concerned with the meanings that may be given to quality indicators.

The two examples show that quality does not result automatically from one dimension of considerations (for example if users are satisfied, quality is good), but rather that there is a *choice* between different criteria: customer expectations, standards determined by the experience of professionals, cost constraints, and specific objectives of the public service. It is very important to remember this because it is possible to slip from a situation where the civil service determines its choice without any consultation, to a situation where choice is purely governed by surveys. However, some services should not be subject to satisfaction ratings alone. In matters of environmental protection, for example, the Ministry of Equipment, in refusing proposals, may be very unpopular with certain fractions of the population. Or again, a school may only indirectly contemplate the satisfaction of students and parents.

The present paradox of the public service is that it needs to look for customer satisfaction and at the same time be aware of the fact that this is not the only relevant criterion. There are two major positions to avoid: basing civil service action exclusively on measures of user satisfaction; and, conversely, allowing civil servants to continue to think that they have a spontaneous and inner knowledge of their customers.

The civil service insists that the customers' point of view is included in its decisions. Yet, essential elements still have to be fully thought through in the field of methodology and social regulation.

First, public service customers are not a homogeneous category: they are divided into different groups with different interests. This problem should not really be compared with testing the quality of products for consumption. Some customers are organized, others are not. Some organizations are in a position to negotiate with officials and to represent a mandate. Other refuse to negotiate or are not trusted or believed in by their members.

Secondly, customers are not facing a company in the market-place, but have the state as their 'supplier'. This is not a neutral but a symbolic and value-laden relationship. A customer of a public service may be reacting not because of a product, but because of a certain idea he or she has of the civil service or the government as a whole. Every public service has its professional complainers. In the same line of reasoning, sociological studies show that progress which is accomplished is frequently immediately forgotten, because implicitly there is no such thing as a limit to the welfare state.

Thirdly, different techniques exist to analyse customers, from survey to semi-structured interviews. It would be helpful to have research which shows in which conditions to implement each of these techniques. Today, the choice of these techniques seems to be determined almost by chance, depending on the choice of experts or the personal preference of the civil servant concerned.

Fourthly, it should be clear that customer involvement tends to create socially conflictual situations with civil servants, as well as political tensions, if their advice is not followed. Is transparency in all circumstances manageable? In particular, there is a delicate equilibrium between on the one hand having civil servants accept that their *a priori* ideas on clients are not necessarily founded on substance, and on the other hand not recognizing their professionalism.

Whether one should let organizations collect data on customers, or give customers the opportunity to express themselves in an autonomous and direct way, does not have a single answer. In the two cases analysed, the two techniques are mixed. There are customer groups as well as surveys and sociological investigations of these customer groups. However, the Ministry of Equipment is a very decentralized organization. Problems in one DDE are not necessarily general problems. France-Télécom too is a diverse organization where it is possible to distinguish between the appreciation of a particular product and the general strategy of the organization. Other organizations, like the Ministry of Education, are confronted with much more difficult questions. A customer group, national or local, may find it hard to distinguish between specific questions on quality and the general direction of the public service. Parents, whilst appreciating school visits to enterprises, may nevertheless question professionalization at school. These organizations invite universalistic definitions of problems. In this case, the role of customer groups is much more complex because there is a threat of a tendency towards a general discussion on the objectives of the organization. There is less room for reflection on quality.

These remarks are not intended to prove that it makes no sense to look at customer expectations. They rather suggest that it is necessary to take additional factors into account.

The Ministry of Equipment and France-Télécom both illustrate the non-neutrality of the customer concept in the public service. There is no such thing as a clear, unique, legitimate demand that one can translate into standards and norms of products. Rather, the reality is of an opaque, multi-shaped demand which is full of conflicting interests. For management this implies:

1 A high level of investment. An analysis of clients of a DDE may represent the equivalent of three or four months of work by a consultant or a graduate.
2 A capacity to manage the conflicts that may appear between civil servants and customers.

Emerging questions

A central question is: who is defining the indicators? Are they imposed by the centre or freely chosen by the services as part of their management? The cases show that it is good to have both types of indicator: general, simple and compulsory indicators, such as delays or degree of preciseness of answers, designed to be accountable to the citizen; and indicators to control quality developed by the services themselves. The first type of indicator should upgrade the traditional principles of the civil service: continuity of service, equity of treatment in equal circumstances, and adaptability. The second type of indicator is meant to motivate civil servants in their relations with the clients.

Nevertheless, it is important to realize that all these indicators cannot be the same because they do not respond to the same needs and they are developed differently. There is *a priori* no reason whatsoever why the indicators that civil servants need to improve their activities should be congruent with the indicators that customers are concerned about. Accountability indicators result from objectives determined by political and managerial authorities, based on *their* appreciation of customer expectations. Quality control indicators result from a civil servant inspired diagnosis of problems existing between the service and its clients, and the internal repercussions of these for the organization. For example, at the national level, the Ministry of Equipment may require its operating units to be accountable for the speed of delivering construction permits (indicator: delay). Yet, at the same time, a DDE at the local level may use an indicator linked to the quality of the explanation of why the permit is positive (agreement) or negative (disagreement) because its clients do not understand the decisions that were taken (indicator: existence of stated reasons for the decision taken).

Is this a superfluous refinement, especially since a major question is to confront client expectations and the public service's objectives? The distinction is useful because it allows differentiation between quasi-compulsory indicators and those that result from an autonomous analysis of the organization. Both are indispensable but not relevant to the same extent, depending on whether one looks at the total organization or at a particular service.

In summary, one could say that accountability quality indicators are:

1 central;
2 compulsory;
3 required by objectives and for the analysis of total demand for an institution (expectations for national education are not the same as for a single school);
4 relevant for information expected by customers
5 quantitative

Quality control indicators imply:

1 an analysis of specific demands of different clients of the organization;
2 problems and dysfunctions (technical quality);

3 local autonomy for appreciation and evaluation;
4 a sense of work utility for civil servants;
5 qualitative indicators (although verifiable).

Is one of the two types of indicator set more extensive or more costly? Investment is significant in both cases. A quality indicator file at France-Télécom takes several months of testing and developing. Organizational sections have to fuel the monthly organizational monitoring system and commit themselves to the reliability of these data. At the Ministry of Equipment the data are not aggregated. This reduces the unreliability of data. Nevertheless, the investment in client analysis and the diagnosis of service dysfunctioning require a considerable intellectual effort. It seems a little artificial to try to measure the cost of quality efforts if the organization ignores the cost of routine activities. However, it should be possible to start measuring their efficiency. If quality efforts are made, client relations improve: the motivation of civil servants increases since they are now capable of responding to questions and criticisms, which was not so much the case before they possessed that information. What is more, quality know-how is not likely suddenly to become obsolete. For many years, the DDEs have taken the direction of working qualitatively. There is as yet no sign of any falling away.

The two cases show that indicators may become efficient only if their is a strong accompanying effort at interpretation. Each indicator has a potential for bias from its initial goal, since the customers for indicators use them for their own purposes. Each indicator has unforeseen effects. Each indicator may support diverging interpretations. For example, an indicator of waiting times at service windows pushes civil servants to a response which is as fast as possible. Yet, this may be to the detriment of the quality of explaining matters to clients. This may cause errors or new steps. The time gained is lost later. It therefore is necessary to put into place a permanent monitoring and analysis mechanism which is accepted by the organization and its staff.

A major lesson France is learning from these experiences is that there is no such thing as a unique quality model: rather there are different methods responding to different objectives. Also, the administration hopes that there will be no more quality circles or total quality exercises. For different reasons, these initiatives did not achieve the expected results. TQM was poorly managed, it was not a sustained effort, and was too much top-down driven.

A prime objective flowing from the current experiences seems to be that of making deconcentrated services responsible. This implies that a distinction is made, from the beginning of the process, between information which is compulsory, and indicators which services are free to develop in the context of better management and improved relationships with clients. The only restriction is that these indicators should match their scheduled objectives. If central organizations wish to possess indicators for reasons of accountability for particular products, such as delivery times, they will have to make explicit how to do this and restrict themselves to significant volumes. Indicators supporting decision-making and controlling are not to be made compulsory by central services experts looking for a technical optimum, but must result from planned objectives and analyses. Through the latter, the central organization should seek to provide advice, synthesis and co-ordination.

5

Quality Improvement in German Local Government

Helmut Klages and the Speyer Award Team of the City of Duisburg

Tension between quality assurance by legal protection of civic rights and by civic participation in Germany

Historical roots and present traces

It seems to be true though paradoxical that the public sectors of developed nations mirror much more of their countries' histories than the public sectors of developing nations (which have often been imported from outside without any reference to local traditions). This general rule holds true for Germany, which without any doubt is a modern nation today, yet possesses an administrative culture which is still quite heavily marked by certain traits from its nineteenth-century history.

When we deal with questions concerning the quality orientation of the German public sector we immediately encounter a quite funda-mental and dominating peculiarity. It may be termed the tension between quality assurance by legal protection of civic rights and quality assurance by civic participation.

In the historical roots of this tension we find a determined tendency to draw sharp distinctions between civil society and the state (Ellwein and Hesse, 1987). The original purpose of this distinction was to be modern concerning the liberal prerequisites of industrial develop-ment, but without sacrificing too much of the political heritage of the ruling elites.

Indeed these elites were enlightened enough to accept a rather high degree of autonomy in local government, which comfortably exceeded the levels that were reached in Great Britain or France. On the other hand the relationship between the public sector and the individual citizen was defined as *hoheitlich*, meaning a unilaterally constructed chain of command and obedience. This was mitigated, however, by very strict rules of accountability of civil servants to an 'administrative law', the creation of which was a typical German achievement. Even today, long after the dissolution of the traditional elites, many German academics are still confusing administrative science with administrative law, because the latter seems to them to be at the very centre of every kind of thinking concerning the public sector. Accordingly *Rechtmäßigkeit* (lawfulness) was the main measure of the 'quality' of the public sector for a long time, being complemented only be *Wirtschaftlichkeit* (economy).

The consequence and intensity of this peculiar path of definition and development can be traced by looking at the legally defined shape and structure of the so-called *Verwaltungsakt*, meaning the standard act of administrative decision-making for individual cases. According to the rules constituting the *Verwaltungsakt*, administrations are entitled to unilateral decision-making concerning the regulation of civic behaviour, wherever an appropriate legal basis can be assumed. On the other hand the citizen concerned can contradict any administrative decision only by using strictly defined rules. The consequence of a contradiction will be that a formalized procedure of control is triggered, which includes going to an administrative court (Wipfler, 1979).

Developments since the 1960s
Since the 1960s the German public sector has been exposed to the same external pressures as others in the developed world, that is to say, among other things, to:

1 a remarkable growth and complexity of tasks;
2 a thoroughgoing societal value change, in the direction of self-actualization;
3 a process of continuous upgrading of participation as a legitimate request of citizens;
4 a necessity to develop capacities for a decentralized way of dealing with problems in order to secure social acceptance and satisfaction;
5 a growing desire by citizens to be able to 'consume' outputs of the public sector in an approximately similar way to those of the private sector, and to experience 'quality' as an output attribute, as well as an attribute of the way in which services are delivered.

The German public sector has been reacting to these pressures in various ways. Given the background it is hardly surprising that, among such adaptations, those which attempt to transfer the traditional pattern of a separation between state and society into the new, altered situation have played an important role.

So, for instance, the conditions of access to administrative courts were improved, so that everybody, be they educated and rich or not, could have a chance to defend themselves against administrative failures and arbitrary acts. Furthermore ombudsmen and/or *Bürgerbeauftragte* (commissioners for citizens' matters) have been installed, who are available for direct access by people having trouble with civil servants and/or public servants and/or public agencies, and who are entitled to intervene in procedures without observing the normal procedural rules.

In view of the strong nature and the culturally based character of the German tradition it has to be regarded as a quite significant development that the late 1960s also brought some advances in the direction of participatory procedures. Laws were enacted which provided for the innovation that citizens afflicted by public city or road planning measures, or, for instance, by plans concerning the establishment of atomic energy plants or garbage incinerators, should have a chance to be heard in an organized way.

On the other hand, the state did not dispense with its traditional insistence on unilateral decision-making. Nevertheless these new laws indicated that the public sector was turning towards a new ideal of 'responsiveness', and that there was growing appreciation of the necessity to build up societal acceptance regardless of the availability of legal justifications.

This change became yet more visible wherever the authorities began to practise what has subsequently been called the *co-operative state*. One of the earliest manifold faces of the co-operative state was the growing readiness of local government agencies to use this latitude, left to them by law in order to secure flexibility, to informally negotiate compromises with diverging social interests, thereby moving very close to the border of unlawful behaviour. In this connection the state did not sacrifice its privilege of unilateral decision-making. It changed its attitude, however, indicating a significantly increased readiness to accept what were in effect outside definitions of quality as parameters to be taken into consideration in the process of decision-making.

At first sight the shell of the German state tradition seemed to fracture when the so-called *Bürgerinitiativen* (civic initiatives) came into being in a sudden landslide at the end of the 1960s. Now a hitherto unthinkable element of spontaneous protest behaviour, striving impatiently for the acquisition of quality in terms of civic wishes and definitions, seemed to penetrate the remote corridors of the authorities. The latter were seemingly to be forced into a new era of participative democracy of the grass-roots type, compelling them to bid farewell to their historically rooted and more or less petrified habits.

With good reason the advent of the civic initiatives received great attention in neighbouring countries. When looking back to this event from the present perspective, as well as from accumulated experience with the still flourishing civic initiatives, one cannot help but qualify first impressions.

To begin with, the hope of many people that the civic initiatives might serve as the seeds of a new type of quality-enforcing grass-roots democracy (see e.g. Grossman, 1971) did not prove to be realistic. Certainly many of the initiatives have been able to intervene in public decision-making and to secure the recognition of previously neglected interests of local groupings of citizens. However, the state of true participation has never been reached. Rather, local governments learned that the variety of manifestations of the co-operative state was greater than they had originally imagined. In other words, they quickly learned that civic initiatives could well be regarded as corrective mechanisms. From a long-range perspective, they increased the chances of the public sector being in accord with societal wishes and desires by flexibly adapting its decision-making activities to what seemed to be, from a short-range perspective, an outburst of hostility. An interpretation from the point of view of German 'state science', which aimed precisely in this direction, was formulated as early as 1970 by Fritz W. Scharpf. Scharpf, amidst a wave of embarrassment triggered by a seemingly mutinous citizenship, pointed to the potential function of indicating possible improvements in the performance of the public sector that the civic initiatives might fulfil (Scharpf, 1970).

Seen from such a perspective it was significant that Peter C. Dienel conceived his famous *Planungszelle* (planning cell). This was an attempt to bring the spontaneity of the civic initiatives within a formalized shape, as an instrument of the authorities, providing them with a chance to organize communication with 'representative' citizens, wherever this seemed to be desirable.

Process- and result-oriented quality assurance within the German public sector

On one hand the German public sector was eager to calm the tension between quality assurance by legal protection of civil rights and that by civic participation through a heightened sensitivity and responsiveness. On the other, since the 1960s it has expended great efforts on improving its internal processes and structures, in order to adapt them to the new challenges.

An early approach towards this goal was the so-called *Gebietsreform* (area reform), which reduced the number of local governments quite dramatically, aiming thereby at making the public sector more efficient and effective. The idea behind this large and long-lasting operation was that bigger local governments meant a better chance for professionalizing the work of civil servants. This idea rested on the basic assumption that professionalization of the civil service would automatically bring about a better quality of output from public services (Wagener, 1969). Parallel to this reform process a so-called *Dienstrechtsreform* (reform of the existing laws on the public service) was planned, the aim of which was simpler and more flexible personnel structures. It failed, however, mainly because of the resistance of some of the unions, which feared that the German *Beamten* might lose the so-called *Lebenszeitprinzip* (tenure principle).

A second approach concentrated on formulating *Sicherheitsstandards und Grenzwerte* (security standards and threshold values) for a growing number of production processes and services also within the private sector, whereby earlier initiatives, which partly went back to the end of the nineteenth century, could be used as a basis. This idea of setting service standards, which has only recently entered the British scene, came into being much earlier in Germany, where it became constrained, however, by the dominating principle of the legal protection of civil rights.

Thirdly, a broad variety of attempts at *Entbürokratisierung* (debureaucratization) were undertaken, among which the following approaches can be discerned:

1 *Rechtsvereinsfachung* (simplification of the law) with a growing tendency towards deregulation;
2 *Vereinfachung der Gesetzessprache* and *Formularvereinfachung* (simplification of the language of laws, rules and forms used by authorities) with the aim to give the ordinary citizen a chance to read and to understand the regulations;
3 improvement of the *Bürgernähe* (closeness to the citizens) of public authorities by decentralizing offices, by giving offices a friendly appearance through making office buildings more transparent, by training civil servants in friendly behaviour to visitors,

by adapting office hours to the time-table of citizens and so on (see Grunow, 1988).

Fourthly, the new information and communication technologies were energetically introduced. The aim was to enable the public services to work faster and with fewer failures, and thereby to improve the quality of the output (see Lenk, 1990; Reinermann, 1986).

On the basis of the new technologies a remarkable organizational innovation has been tested over many years, which seems to be a German peculiarity, and possible a German export. This is the so-called *Bürgerämter* and *Bürgerbüros* (citizen's offices and citizen's bureaux), which are presently mushrooming at the local level. At the very centre of this innovation resides the idea that citizens visiting such an office should have the opportunity to address any civil servant who is present with any personal request, without being forced to search for a specialist who is 'in charge'.

It is quite clear that in a culture with an extremely differentiated and opaque legal structure, such an innovation means an enormous improvement in the quality of the citizen's interaction with the public sector. The German public sector is crossing another river by introducing this innovation. It is beginning to internalize the informational burden, which follows from the peculiar shape of the national legal structure, thus accepting a formidable task.

In view of this evolution, heightened attention to personnel development seems a 'must'. Personnel development is a fifth aspect of quality-oriented public sector modernization, which – after some hesitation – has recently begun to flourish in Germany. Whilst it is true that there have not been dramatic breakthroughs in this field up to now, its seems reasonable to predict such a breakthrough in the near future.

The sixth current development is of particular importance because it is the first clear case of Germany borrowing from its western neighbours. After some drumming by the *Gemeinschaftsstelle für Verwaltungsvereinfachung*, several German cities have begun to introduce internal contract management as a new steering philosophy, whereby they explicitly take developments in the Netherlands as a model.

In close connection with this significant change a seventh trend can be observed which concerns the introduction of *controlling* into the toolbox of public management. At this point performance measurement, which until quite recently was largely reserved for juridical procedures aimed at the control of the authorities' adherence to normative prescriptions, enters the scene.

Recent signals from the participation frontier in Germany

It can be taken from the foregoing that the traditional adherence of the German public sector to the principle of unilateral decision-making did not prevent it from investing a growing amount of energy in an internal modernization process. As we saw at the end of the previous chapter, this process has now reached a stage at which immediate borrowings from other countries' developments have become possible. In other words, the uniqueness of the German situation is fading, although there can be no doubt as to its continuing consciousness. The German public sector – notwithstanding the fact that it is still marked by distinctive traditions – is opening up to various strands of innovation.

Although the signals may be regarded as ambiguous, a trend to approximate 'participative' solutions can be observed. Thus in the German context it has to be regarded as significant that the *Verwaltungsrechtslehre* (administrative law as a discipline) has for some time been exploring the possibilities for integrating a 'dialogical' communication with citizens into the legal basis of administrative activity (see Pitschas, 1990).

The most important practical development seems to be a progressive amplification of the understanding of the term *co-operative state*, which has already been discussed above. Originally this term covered only public decision-making in consideration of societal interests against the background of laws and rules as preset frames. However, it now encompasses several approaches to joint public/private decision-making, which may even aim interactively to create new norms and rules which are appropriate to meet quality-oriented expectations from outside (see Hill, 1993).

In truth, ordinary citizens are not likely to participate in the relevant decision-making circles. These will rather be the meeting-points (or the 'round tables') of organized actors. However, some cities in Nordrhein-Westfalia have also begun to carry out regular surveys.

We are aware of the criticism that can be levelled at surveys (see e.g. Blackman, 1992). We suggest, however, that this criticism overlooks the limitations of interactively proceeding with quality definition and evaluation procedures unless they are open to everybody. Also, we think that such criticism cannot be transferred from system to system without reflecting the differing system-specific frameworks, as well as the diverging possibilities bound up with them. In Germany regular surveys aimed at measuring the outcomes of administrative systems in terms of the satisfaction and dissatisfaction of their addressees may be regarded as a revolutionary innovation.

Of course, one may theorize that a complete system of outcome measurement and evaluation ought to go well beyond surveys. Surveys might well be combined, for instance, with planning cells (see above) and other kinds of direct interaction. It has to be acknowledged, however, that we are in the realm of futuristic thinking when we construct such combined systems. Furthermore it may be that the process of the internal modernization of the German public sector is, at its present stage, rather resistant to direct interaction. In theory there should not be a contradiction between internal and external aspects of the modernization process. Nevertheless it is possible that administrative systems which follow a 'hybridization' strategy of public sector modernization (Klages and Haubner, 1995), will proceed through stages of development that may be connected in a 'dialectic' way.

We think that it is necessary to take such a realistic point of view, between the extremes, as we now turn to a German local authority case study. This example displays the development of a quality-oriented public service system right at the frontier of what is currently seen as possible in Germany.

Short description of Duisburg

Duisburg is a large city with a population of 540,000, situated at the western edge of the Ruhr area, where the Ruhr flows into the Rhine. The decline of the steel industry over the last 20 years has led to major job losses in Duisburg, resulting in a population outflow of about 100,000 people. As a result the city of Duisburg was forced to implement cost-cutting programmes involving a reduction of local infrastructure. Mastering structural change is the topic that dominates local government development policy.

Duisburg may be helped in its development by its favoured position in relation to transport routes and facilities. Duisburg has the largest European inland port and is located on busy north–south and east–west railway lines and roads.

The local government has a staff of about 9,500, while local-authority-controlled organizations employ another 8,000 people.

Local government structure in Duisburg is characterized by the fact that citizen-oriented services are offered from seven highly independent district offices close to the target groups. In political terms, Duisburg has for many years had a social democratic tradition, supported by workers, with solid majorities in the city council.

In the future Duisberg – like all local governments in Germany – will have to carry the heavy financial burden of the 'solidarity pact' for the reconstruction of East Germany. This is why a new consolidation programme has already been initiated.

Local government reform in Duisberg

In promoting structural change Duisberg was particularly dependent on the co-operation of all those concerned. Major projects aiming to improve the economic structure include using the inland port as a free port and setting up a multi-functional service centre as well as designating new industrial precincts in combination with a technology park and a business park.

These projects could only be realized with contributions by the federal and state governments, large banks and local chambers of commerce and industrial associations. Local government fulfilled a very important function in initiating and channelling industrial initiatives and in cross-linking different types of organizations involved in development.

This strengthened the conviction of local government leaders that local government needed to adopt the *role* of a local service industry. This feature needs to be expressed both in its external customer orientation and in its internal management structure.

This is why Duisburg has made special efforts with the way in which it communicates with the general public, as well as in gearing its services to specific target groups, providing staff in-service training and adapting its control tools.

Quality improvement in the city of Duisburg

Cultural and internal prerequisites

The city administration of Duisburg regards itself as a modern service establishment in its co-operative relationships with citizens, the economy, science and social institutions on the outside, and in its direction by an up-to-date and purpose-oriented management on the inside. Challenges which arise from this basic understanding include:

1 accepting changes in the values held by its citizens and employees;
2 accepting changes in the regional economic structure;
3 being recognized as a driving force in helping authorities to adapt themselves to being modern service establishments.

In the following, the aims and effects of selected measures from the fields of personnel, organization and resources, finance, economic feasibility and supervision, and external relations will be identified and contrasted with each other.

Personnel
The employees are found at the heart of the change processes. In Duisburg they are both the organizers of the changes and those affected by them. For this reason, there is no particular focus on human resource investments – according to requirements and also anticyclical personnel policy – in the following areas:

1 selection;
2 training;
3 informing of employees;
4 advanced training;
5 motivation.

The afore-mentioned programme simultaneously takes into consideration the demographic development, the diminishing employment market, the half-life period of knowledge and the expectations of young new employees. Its consequent translation does not serve merely to raise the general level of qualifications, but is equally able to improve the information and motivations of staff.

In order to maintain a consolidated information base for the orientation of a personnel development programme, all employees will be consulted at regular intervals. The collected data will be supplemented with annual discussions between employees and their superiors. These discussions will form the most important constituents of a dialogue with the employees to emphasize the importance of a 'co-operative organization'.

In addition, individual programmes will also be promoted and regularly checked for their success rate, for example the opportunities for women to attain leading positions. Support will also be given to people re-embarking on their careers.

The significance for a modern service establishment of the

employees' competence in their specialized field, and of their social competence, shapes the form of 'assessment-centred' selection procedures on the one hand and the focus on guided training on the other. Strategic guidance for a co-operative organization will be modulated as an instrument to be used in concrete guidance practices, and further development. Alongside the availability of information at all levels, there is a willingness to trust in co-operation and to treat conflicts not in a formal way, but rather in a manner that is primarily oriented to achieving an aim or solution.

An important aim of all the efforts is the development of the employees' basic communal understanding of the 'enterprise city' as well as in the development of a uniform maxim of action. As a result, it is also important that personnel and organization development measures are conceptually integrated. They will form the self-evident instruments of a modern, quality-oriented administrative management.

To sum up, the following measures and field of activity may give an impression of the modernization of the personnel field in Duisburg:

1 new personnel selection procedures in the training field;
2 seminar programmes relating to the scope of the practical training;
3 focal points within specialized advanced training;
4 technical emphasis to the advanced training regarding key qualifications;
5 guided training in administrative management;
6 new personnel selection procedures for prominent positions;
7 strategic administrative leadership;
8 an aim of developing an innovative administrative culture;
9 a 'round table' with personnel advisers and trade unions;
10 introduction of regularly occurring discussions with employees;
11 the development of a corporate identity and corporate design.

Organization and resources
Administrative work in the communal sector can be *assessed* by the public as to whether it is carried out sufficiently quickly, individually, locally and within reasonable expenditure. A clear competence that is visible at a glance will be promoted in this way. In Duisburg, a matrix organization has been chosen for this purpose, with separate sections to carry out planning and the execution of the entire set of municipal duties, to provide supervision through central offices and to carry out duties through district offices.

Local services are supplied through seven city district offices. Extensive competence in decision-making, common approaches to the citizens and limited interference by professional supervision result in 'shorter paths'. By combining the duties and work of the city district under one roof, more responsive work procedures and decisions are made possible. In addition, public information offices provide a comprehensive overall view of the services being offered and of the competence of the city administration.

In order to improve work procedures and working conditions for the employees and to meet the requirements of the citizens whilst nevertheless observing the need to economize, cost efficient administrative work procedures are planned and carried out which continually incorporate the expectations of the employees. This secures the employees' identification with the organizational solutions and increases service productivity. Project organization is an additional aid in conducting complex duties in an individual, economic, cooperative and task-oriented way, without the need for constant alterations in the administrative organization.

Available information and an exploitation of information technology are decisive elements for comprehensive and cost efficient administrative work. For this purpose, comprehensive technological support for information processing has been developed. This will be reassessed at regular intervals, taking account of strategically significant conditions and trends. A decentralized information processing concept has been employed in order to create integrated solutions relating employment positions with communication feasibilities.

Finances, economic feasibility and supervision
The community, social and political objectives of the communal action programme are not exempt from the requirement for economy. On the contrary, the allocation of public resources on the basis of trust (rather than for a specific purpose) by the public demands the greatest possible efficiency and effectiveness.

The methods by which Duisburg attempts to meet these expectations are purposeful, cost-aware management and guidance with the help of individual matched controlling instruments based on careful financial planning. In this regard, the previous practice of centralized management of the essential resources of money and personnel had a rather negative effect. As a consequence a decentralization of business and resource responsibilities was intended to bring about an awareness of the inseparable connection between duty and cost in self-contained fields of responsibility.

Classified areas and areas that have been transferred into private hands will be linked to the objectives of an *enterprise city* through participative administration. This *supervision* will deliver the necessary information to the council and heads of the administration, who in turn will guide the entire administrative system. In this context the measures employed include:

1 detailed financial planning;
2 a new form for the budget structural allowance;
3 decentralized controlling systems;
4 economic feasibility controlled by identified stages;
5 construction of an intercommunal indicator system;
6 evaluation methods focusing on suitability and economic feasibility.

External relations
The 'service enterprise' city is shaped on the one hand by a critical public, and on the other by the realization that the European market means increasing international competition. A communal and social political objective will be consequently developed according to the requirements and expectations of the public, and a fixed profile will be shaped. This will be enabled by an intensive dialogue with the public, with the responsible parties in the economy, science, politics and other associations, and also through a consistent project-oriented policy of co-operation.

This co-operation carries a regional and a strong European accent. First, it requires the opening up of the administration. In this way 'administration' will come to be more than the regional profile representative of previous years. This will be supported by the development of a concept that should lead to a coherent public image of the city of Duisburg. In this context, we have to look at the following instruments:

1 consultations with the public at regular intervals;
2 image analysis;
3 conference for public work;
4 economic support for a public/private partnership;
5 investors and image campaigns.

Note

The Speyer Award Team includes J. Bickenbach, Th. Lambertz, W. Lappe, J. Siemens and E. Splitt.

6

Quality Improvement in Local Service Contracts: Environmental Services in Harlow

Lucy Gaster

This case study, of one local authority's neighbourhood approach to quality in contracts, demonstrates how local users and citizens can become involved in defining and monitoring quality. In the relatively simple service area of the local environment, it illustrates the complexity of the contractual system, showing how the triangular relationship of consumer, contractor and client representative can be helped or hindered by the attitudes and behaviour of one or more of the parties. A weak link in the 'service chain' affects the quality of the whole.

The starting point for this case study (carried out in March 1993) is Harlow District Council's commitment, under the banner of 'decentralization and democratization', both to decentralized access to services and to local participative democracy. The council has consequently developed neighbourhood offices and area committees. The implementation strategy also included the innovative appointment of neighbourhood-based environmental inspectors: these have proved to be a vital element in the local approach to developing quality in contracts.

The potential role of the local consumer and resident

In local government, residents are citizens and they may be consumers. These roles affect their relationship with services and with service quality in different ways.

Citizen rights are derived from people's roles as voters and taxpayers. These rights include: being informed, heard and listened to, and receiving explanation (Steward and Ranson, 1994). They can, of course, only be exercised if those with power – the elected body – agree that they exist and if appropriate structures for consultation and participation are in place.

At the same time, local residents may be consumers or customers.

While the ideal model for the improvement of quality in public services might expect the power of providers and 'customers' to be more or less equal, in many services an even-handed relationship is extremely difficult to achieve. Power rests so strongly with the producer that the notion of 'customer' as an individual with the right to choose whether to receive services (and to withdraw from them if they are not satisfactory) is simply irrelevant. People will not see themselves as 'customers' while the built-in power of professionals and the dominating tendencies of bureaucracy persist. At the same time, factors such as stigma, powerlessness within society, and the very nature of the services provided lead to unequal relationships.

The nature of the service is important. In local government, it is possible to distinguish between four broad categories, each of which has rather different implications for the producer–consumer relationship. It might be argued that the distinction between these categories is becoming blurred with the introduction of market mechanisms. The division between 'purchaser', 'commissioner' or 'client' roles on the one hand, and 'provider' or 'contractor' roles on the other, is intended by central government to produce more choice, as well as more efficient services. This is not the place to analyse the effectiveness of these 'quasi-market' mechanisms (see Le Grand and Bartlett, 1993). However, local residents have not become 'customers' by the stroke of the contractual pen. The real power of the individual who needs or receives the service has, if anything, been weakened, not enhanced. This is why the Harlow experience, where there is a real attempt to counteract the exclusion of local residents from the contract process, is particularly interesting.

Table 6.1 shows how examples of local government services can be classified. Some services are provided to the whole community; some may be overtly rationed where demand greatly exceeds supply; some are 'compulsory', whether because of national legislation or because of local rules and regulations; and some are provided for residents to use or not, as they wish, sometimes for payment, sometimes free at the point of delivery. Most if not all local government services can be placed in one of these four categories, all of which (except the first) will – or should – have relationships not only with current users or consumers, but also with excluded, past or potential consumers.

It is useful to locate the service whose quality is being discussed within this spectrum and to identify the democratic structures in place that affect people's rights as consumers and citizens. The likely balance – or imbalance – of power between those providing the services and those needing, wanting or receiving them can be

Table 6.1   *Type of service in local government*

Type of service	Examples
Universal	Street cleaning; rubbish collection; environmental services
Rationed	Housing services; home help; benefits
Compulsory	Legally enforced services: planning applications; mental health sections; environmental health actions
Choice	Services for which charge is made (e.g. leisure, day nurseries); services free at point of delivery (e.g. libraries, parks)

identified and, where necessary, steps can be taken to redress that balance.

The environmental services in this case study are 'universal' services: individuals have no choice as to whether they will receive them. There is no overt individual rationing, nor is there any element of personal compulsion. Universal does not, however, mean uniform, and balances need to be struck between what is desirable and what is feasible within the resources available. In addition, as we shall see, choices exist as to what the service consists of and how it is delivered.

Environmental services are, on the whole, collective services. There may be variations or even discrimination between areas (such as the number of dustbin collections). However, disempowerment arising from differences of, say, social class, ethnic origin or disability are less likely than in many of the more personal services where collective weakness may be reinforced by the far greater personal and professional power of the service provider. Given the right circumstances, the power relationship between producer and consumer, between council and citizen, could be reasonably even.

The organizational context in Harlow

In order to achieve a balance of power, effective channels of communication and consultation need to exist. Managerial and political structures must enable the voice of the consumer to be heard and to have influence.

In Harlow, such structures are in place. This is because, since 1989, a policy of 'decentralization and democratization', involving the establishment of neighbourhood offices and area committees, has been evolving (Gaster, 1993). There is a long way to go (indeed, the end is far from clear, as councillors and officers there would agree),

Table 6.2   *Harlow neighbourhood office services and activities*

Services provided within the office
Information and advice about all council services and about other services in the locality
Cash office for rents, council tax etc.
Housing management and advice
Neighbourhood inspector (environmental services)
First point of contact for all services and for making complaints

Services provided elsewhere within the neighbourhood
Differs according to neighbourhood; typically includes contract services such as housing repairs and environmental services (likely to 'drop in'); family and community centres; leisure facilities (any or all may be represented on neighbourhood management team)

Back-line services provided through neighbourhood surgeries, telephone and technology links etc.
Planning, environmental health, welfare benefits, specialist advice; community development; corporate services (legal, personnel, client services)

Strategic activities
Supporting residents' and users' associations; area committees of councillors; local service plans; local service quality promises; delivering corporate policies; liaison with statutory and voluntary bodies providing local services (health, social services etc.)

---

but structures have already emerged that both allow individuals better access to services and encourage collective consideration of local priorities and service quality. (For a fuller discussion of the relationships between quality, decentralization and devolution, see Gaster, 1992.)

Individual access: neighbourhood offices
In a town of 74,000 population, eight neighbourhood offices will eventually provide all residents and local businesses with extremely local individual access to the council. Services include a cash facility, most housing management services, information and advice, the right of referral to other council services and a channel for complaints. In each area, a neighbourhood services manager co-ordinates all the services affecting the area, including those provided by new corporate support service units (replacing the old departments). In the words of one such manager, they also increasingly act as the local 'enabler', bringing together a whole range of bodies, statutory, community and voluntary, for the benefit of the local community. For the range of services that may be provided from or through the neighbourhood offices, see Table 6.2.

The development of commitment and loyalty to the neighbour-hood is an innovative way of working that does not suit everyone: 'our [local] priorities are not their [central department] priorities' said one local worker. But it provides the opportunity to provide services 'according to what people wanted, not just what the council was offering'.

Collective debate: mechanisms of participative democracy
Knowing what people want is achieved in three ways: developing local knowledge; community development; and new consultation mechanisms.

Knowledge of the area and of the local community is built up among front-line staff, through contact with members of the public who visit or phone the office, or by going out and talking to local residents. If the organizational culture values front-line staff, their local knowledge can be fed into decision-making and policy formu-lation. A cultural shift of this nature is perceptible in Harlow. It is quite uneven, however, causing some tensions between centre and locality in different areas of work and affecting the amount of influence on the centre from the neighbourhoods.

Secondly, in Harlow, neighbourhood offices have a specific remit to help develop the community as a community, sometimes with the help of community development workers (but there are never enough of them), sometimes by working with existing or embryo groups of residents. Where there are enough groups – in the neighbourhood studied for this case study for example – they come together as a 'neighbourhood forum'. This, joined by representatives of local churches, schools and so on, has considerable legitimacy to speak for the community as a whole. It can be consulted about specific and sometimes quite technical issues: capital schemes, planning applications and the council's budgetary situation. It is also a channel for discussion of contract specifications, as we shall see.

Thirdly, the councillors (Labour Party majority) have reorganized their committee system to emphasize the role of neighbourhoods. They have abolished traditional service committees such as for housing, planning or leisure and established area committees, backed by central strategic and policy committees for the develop-ment and monitoring of corporate policy frameworks. At the same time, budgets are beginning to move to an area basis. This means that major decisions can be taken locally, and that an area perspective can be built into district-wide issues. The stated eventual aim is to *empower* local people. The intermediate positions is that local people are beginning to be *heard* and *to be involved*.

Improving the environment
In Harlow, environmental contracts arising from the compulsory competitive tendering legislation have been phased in since 1989, at about the same time as the neighbourhood initiative got off the ground. The idea of monitoring the contracts through generic community inspectors emerged. They were to act as local agents of 'the client', initially as a short-term, monitored 'experiment'. The first inspectors were appointed in 1990.

The tasks were: formally and systematically to monitor the grounds maintenance, refuse collection and street cleansing contracts; to be 'the eyes and ears' of the neighbourhood for a whole range of other issues, such as broken pavements, damaged street lights and dead animals; and, by developing positive links with the local community, 'to lessen the effects of what was a complaints-led service and to show that the council cares about the services it provides'. After only six months, the experiment was judged a success, financially and in terms of improved quality control and quality assurance.

An infrastructure for quality
In an organization which now has an explicit and developed corporate approach to improving the quality of all its services, these factors provide a solid starting point – an infrastructure – for detailed quality initiatives. Since this would be almost too rational, it is unsurprising that in practice each policy strand – the decentralization and democratization, the quality policy and the ideas about contract monitoring – developed separately. It was only as they started taking root and were 'owned' at key political and managerial levels that the connections began to be made. By 1993, they were explicitly seen as interlocking dimensions of an overall policy of opening up the council and enhancing local democracy.

Issues arising

This case study provides an example of several of the dimensions of quality. They include:

1 how quality is defined in the different contracts and in day-to-day practice;

2 how users and residents and front-line staff are involved in contract specification;
3 how users and residents are involved in monitoring and contract compliance;
4 the impact of budget restrictions, that is, quality may sometimes be about looking for alternative methods of service delivery.

The following sections refer both to research undertaken in Harlow generally and to a more detailed study at a particular neighbourhood.

Definitions of quality
Referring to grounds maintenance, the neighbourhood inspector interviewed for this study commented: 'I want my grass cut, I want the litter out of my [flower] bed, I want my hedge cut every October – that's what people want!'

Definitions of quality are, however, rather more complicated, not only because the contracting organization needs to know what is required, but so that the client organization knows what to expect and, when necessary, to enforce. In contracts, quality can be formally defined, in the sense that both process and outputs are written into the specification. Equally, quality may be demonstrated in the choice, flexibility and responsiveness available in practice during implementation (Walsh, 1993).

For the environmental contracts discussed here – covering street cleansing and highways maintenance, waste collection and grounds maintenance – legislation (for example, the Environmental Protection Act) lays down some minimum standards. Thus councils know how much litter is 'acceptable' in residential compared with shopping areas. For highways maintenance, the lower-tier district council acts (and itself competes annually for the job) as the agent of the county council: when drawing up the specification for its own contractors, it is therefore subject to some county-wide requirements. And for all the contracts being discussed here, it is safe to say that there was, when the new legislation requiring external contracting came into force, a strong motivation to draw them up in such a way as to favour the in-house direct services organizations (DSOs) (which, so far, have indeed won the contracts). So job protection, not service quality, was the early priority, and the contract specifications in force at the time of this study (spring 1993) were drawn up entirely by the council (officers and councillors), subject to the constraints just described.

The qualitative aspects of these contracts therefore tended to be defined in broad terms. For example, the refuse collection tender document stated that:

> Contractors . . . should be able to demonstrate their intentions to adopt or to move towards . . . delivering quality services to the community.
> (a) Resources: to employ the quality of personnel capable of fulfilling contracts in terms of numbers, qualifications and organisation.
> (b) Quality of service: to have a plan or policy to achieve or monitor quality management systems in carrying out work.

Perhaps the key clauses in this document are those that hint at some of the bad working practices of the past, probably identified through councillors' surgeries and past complaints:

> declare as unsatisfactory workmanship such practices as non-return of emptied bins or lids to the storage point, throwing bags up and down basements, leap-frogging and missed collections, non-closure of gates and doors and similar activities.

Redefinition of contracts: involvement of users and residents

In practice, the contracts have become redefined as they were implemented, both through the development of neighbourhood 'service promises' and through the day-to-day relationship between the neighbourhood inspector and the contractors working locally.

Specific local needs began to be taken into account, and the range of stakeholders widened to include local groups and the neighbourhood forum. At the same time, individual consumers became involved through their contact with the neighbourhood inspectors 'walking the patch' or by visits to the neighbourhood office. 'It was a fairly straightforward task of including what the neighbourhood thought was important.'

Taking street cleansing and rubbish collection, a wide range of quality improvements could be incorporated in practice, thanks to contracts where variation had been anticipated and built in. Examples in the neighbourhood studied have included helping disabled people to get their bins out; picking up extra rubbish; quick and easy dissemination of information about changes to the timetable (such as on public holidays); careful location of special schemes such as recycling for maximum benefit and minimum disturbance. Such definitions include not only the 'technical' aspects of the jobs, but also how they are done – the interactive dimension of quality that always has the potential either to enhance or to undermine the technical quality.

This experience can be used for planning future services. In this neighbourhood, a new housing scheme came on stream. Services were being planned for it, and the local knowledge of the neighbourhood inspector 'shone through' in negotiations with planners, client and contractor departments and residents.

In another example, two neighbourhoods bargained for – and got – 'beat sweepers'. These are street sweepers who, rather than working with a gang right across the town, are dedicated to a single neighbourhood, with a rota worked out locally, in consultation with local residents' associations. This gives tremendous flexibility to deal with unforeseen problems. Like the inspectors themselves, the street sweepers become very well known locally, and their integration with the neighbourhood team, as yet one more source of information about local needs, and one more outlet for information about the council, has been much appreciated. The system is now to be extended to other neighbourhoods.

A cyclical process of definition

The contracts have provided a bottom line for basic quality definitions and for monitoring delivery, both by the neighbourhood inspector and by the public. However, through a process of local dialogue, formal and informal, a clearer picture of the particular needs of the neighbourhood has been built up. Rather than waiting for the next round of contract specification (see below), it has proved possible in the neighbourhood studied for the local office, backed by the area committee of councillors, to develop a local service standard, negotiated with the neighbourhood forum and the client service officers and published as the neighbourhood 'service promise'. This leads to an evolving definition of quality, an ongoing process of monitoring and redefinition. It also provides the starting point for the neighbourhood to feed its experience into the formal process of contract specification for the next round of contracts.

The impact of budget restrictions

While the quality of the work carried out under contract can be improved through enhanced sensitivity to local needs, other influences may lead in the opposite direction. The most obvious of these, one that was impinging on Harlow at the time of the study, is a threatened or actual reduction in resources.

Where a contract is drawn up in quite broad terms, and where there is room for local variance within the meaning of the contract, and where dialogue and trust have been established between the local office and the local community, alliances of local councillors, officers and the public can be formed and can strengthen the debate. In the neighbourhood being studied, for example, the threat of the street sweeper being removed was withdrawn after it became clear from local discussions that this was an extremely high priority for the neighbourhood. The cuts fell elsewhere, mainly on centrally located middle management and policy units.

However, with regard to grounds maintenance, two factors made this approach to local quality difficult. First, the original contract was incredibly detailed, with the work required for each small plot of land being specified to an extraordinary degree (including the desired height of the grass in centimetres!). It turned out that this detail was sometimes inaccurate (such as wrong measurements) and, because of labour shortages, unworkable. The inspectors were required to submit weekly monitoring reports, but the time came when the contractors found it impossible to act on them. Moreover, the contract variations were so numerous and technical that it was hardly possible for the inspectors, let alone local people, to carry out effective monitoring anyway. At the time of writing, the contract was suspended.

Secondly, the somewhat entrenched attitude of the client department, the old Leisure Department (now the Landscape and Open Spaces Corporate Support Service), had denied the possibility of constructive involvement of neighbourhoods. The latter had no direct access to management information and were therefore dependent on goodwill and influence, having no actual control. At the same time, decisions with a direct bearing on local people's lives were made without consultation either with the neighbourhood staff or with the local residents. One example was the withdrawal of the well-established service of helping old or disabled people with their gardens. Another was a decision to save money by cutting grass less frequently – and it was the large spaces, least easy to be kept up with voluntary efforts but most needed for children's play, that were to suffer most. Neighbourhood staff thought this was to save machinery maintenance costs.

The neighbourhood perspective was twofold. First, people felt that with due warning, it might have been possible to put an alternative into place before the private garden scheme was withdrawn: indeed they were currently talking with the local college of further education, in the hope of identifying local people who could do the work for a small fee. A search for volunteers had already failed.

Secondly, they feared that the grass-cutting issue would now have to be taken, publicly and formally, to the area committee, rather than being amicably negotiated at local level. Both these actions would, inevitably, be preceded by an avalanche of complaints, just when a measure of trust was beginning to be built up between council and community.

No one denied the council's right to make bottom-line decisions. It was *how* these decisions were made that come in for criticism, and the fact that they could well cause long-term damage to the corporate policies for quality and consultation.

Contract specification: involvement of the neighbourhood

As already mentioned, at the time of the study, work was beginning on the next round of contracts, and specifications were beginning to be drawn up. In Harlow, residents and front-line staff has different opportunities to become involved in the process of contract specification and the definition of quality within contracts, depending on the type of contract. Partly this was due to the legal and other constraints mentioned earlier, partly because of resistance within the organization at central policy level. These factors appeared to be preventing neighbourhood involvement in both the grounds maintenance and the highways contracts.

For street sweeping and refuse collection, however, it was a different story. Here the local co-operation was reflected in new attitudes at all levels within the contractor department, the Cleansing and Environmental Service. The British Standard BS 5750 has been achieved by the refuse collection service and, although this is, as the manager there said, 'only about procedures, not about what the customer perceives as quality', in this case it did signify a real commitment to quality, not just to getting a piece of paper that would help win the contract next time.

So the quality of the service was being pursued through the neighbourhoods. Whereas the existing contract had been drawn up 'tightly', with jobs preservation in mind, this time the emphasis would be on neighbourhood needs:

> The neighbourhood approach will help improve services over time. (DSO manager)

> You can see that [the neighbourhood] influence more and more, in that it determines future decisions – not necessarily that it directly affects the specification because there are other considerations, for example, resources. (neighbourhood services manager)

In practice, the influence is probably exerted in different ways. The direct outcome of the neighbourhood inspector's monitoring and routing of local complaints means that there is more feedback than ever before about how the current contract is being implemented. The appointment of beat road sweepers increases direct account- ability through visibility. The attendance of the neighbourhood inspector at residents' groups and the neighbourhood forum, 'to get feedback and build relationships', means that a broader view of services can be gathered. At the same time, the responsibilities of local residents – to separate out broken glass and to help identify 'trouble spots' – are clarified.

These issues can all be fed through to the corporate services with overall responsibility for the contract, as well as to the contractors themselves for day-to-day improvements. Constructive relation- ships, across and up and down the organization, are the key, quite clearly, to the success in some areas (and the relative failure in others) in achieving a neighbourhood definition of quality.

However, even if informal consultation was not achieved (as in the grounds maintenance example), the draft specification was likely to go out for formal consultation through the neighbourhood forum and the area committee when the time came, because of the council's commitment to the neighbourhood approach.

Lessons from the case study

The neighbourhood approach, which includes both the estab- lishment of neighbourhood offices with a remit to build relationships with the community, and encouragement and support for local participative mechanisms, provides a foundation for local quality initiatives. The appointment of dedicated staff – the neighbourhood inspector – provides the channel between residents and the client and contractor departments. Because the services are 'universal' (see Table 6.1) and not subject to much choice, market mechanisms do not apply: the need for effective consultation and participation are all the greater.

The opportunities for local people to influence the quality of local environmental services are:

1 working informally with the neighbourhood inspector, or formally through the complaints system, to identify non-compliance with the existing contract;
2 developing a local dialogue where specific local needs and priorities can be identified and negotiated;
3 eventually, playing an active role, through formal consultation

mechanisms, in drawing up future, neighbourhood-oriented contract specifications and controlling variations.

While formal mechanisms and the appointment of dedicated staff are important, the key to developing the kind of flexibility needed to meet unanticipated and changing needs is undoubtedly the ongoing and increasingly well-informed day-to-day dialogue with local people, individually and collectively, through local groups and the neighbourhood forum. The main agents for this have been the neighbourhood-based officers rather than the councillors, who have so far reserved their energies for the more formal consultations. Not only does the public have to learn to trust council officers, so do the councillors.

Despite the levels of commitment and understanding to be found in this case study, the development of high quality in local environmental services has not been straightforward. The main problems that have emerged are:

1 The original contracts are complex and tight, inhibiting local flexibility or responsiveness.
2 Some client and some contractor departments have bureaucratic attitudes.
3 Change takes a long time and, as new people are brought into the process, continually needs to be renewed. This requires a lot of energy and hard work, as well as clear policy frameworks that legitimate the role of local people and front-line staff. The result is unevenness in implementation and setbacks in progress. The debate has constantly to be renewed and the culture of user and citizen involvement reinforced.

Many of the points raised in this chapter are applicable to other services: a great deal depends on the infrastructure for quality and participation. Indeed, in Harlow, many more services than just those affecting the environment are being debated in this way. For universal environmental services, however, there are some particular advantages of a participative approach to quality. First, the balance of power between users, residents and the council in relation to environmental services is – or can be – more even than is likely in the context of rationed or compulsory services. Secondly, while specifications can be very technical (using Latin plant names, for example), it is more likely that people in the community are knowledgeable and confident enough to challenge the professionals than they would be in, for example, an acute hospital ward or when applying for housing benefit.

The commitment of local staff, and eventually the council as a whole, to working *with* local people to understand their needs, not 'doing things *to* them', is a key factor in promoting trusting and constructive relationships between council and community and in providing a basis for user-led quality. In a cyclical process, the quality of some services has been both defined and monitored through working in co-operation with neighbourhood residents and a cross-section of staff. This in turn has produced better understanding of local needs by those situated further away from the front line. It is the detailed, day-to-day work that has provided the lubrication for the grand strategy, which would otherwise have remained no more than paper policies.

7

Quality in Swedish Higher Education: a Pilot Study

Hellen Westlund

Like beauty, quality is said to be 'in the eyes of the beholder', meaning that it cannot easily be defined in objective terms. In the service management literature the assessment of service quality is conceived as being based on the customer's comparison of the expected service with the experienced service (Zeithmel et al., 1990). Even if it is accepted that the perception of quality is entirely with the customer, higher education raises the further problem of having several very different groups of customers/users: the students, the potential employers and the society. There is a high probability that the different customer groups have their own spectrum of expectations and thus it becomes difficult for the educator to find a common denominator or, beyond that, to prioritize. Finally, it is not always possible for the users to articulate their needs because the character of the product is to a large extent technically advanced and complex, and therefore not well understood in advance. This phenomenon is sometimes pointed out by the analogy that it would have been impossible to desire work by Beethoven before it existed.

Nevertheless, there are researchers in close contact with the industrial sector who argue that even the quality of a service is a blend of objective factors and subjective judgement (e.g. Gummesson, 1993). Certainly, many people within the academic sector are of the opinion that quality in education has many dimensions that cannot be objectively specified.

Therefore when the assignment to study the quality of higher education in business administration in Sweden was given in 1989, the discussion was initially very confused. A learning process began and is still going on. In this chapter the aim is to describe the complete process of the quality study from its origins to its self-evaluation and finally to an external appraisal. The chapter ends with a discussion of the shortcomings of the study and of plans for the next round.

The origin of the study

The study was initiated by the Universities of Lund and Gothenburg in preparation for the competitive environment which was anticipated within higher education as a result of new government policy. The organization of the task was given to the departments of education of the two universities, in collaboration with the Swedish Central Board of Higher Education (UHÄ). The decision was for a pilot study including a self-evaluation and an external expert audit. This design was borrowed from Holland. Two more schools were included for comparison, namely those in Karlstad and Växjö. The administration at the different institutions was not particularly complex. An individual from each of the participating schools was chosen to form a task group to run the operations. General business administration (BA) was selected as one of the areas for study and the author was a member of the task group.

The aim of the study

The aims of the BA study were formulated by the task group as follows:

1 to be of positive value to the quality efforts in each organization;
2 to permit comparisons between the organizations so as to enhance learning from each other.

At the time the UHÄ centrally prescribed the goals for each department in terms like 'knowledge of', 'ability to' and so on. No other official goals existed. The next level at which goals were articulated was for the individual courses, where objectives were formulated in similar terms and along the same dimensions as the departmental goals. There were no objectives given for other dimensions outside the subject matter (such as for the reputation of the school or for internal support activities). Neither was attention paid to the communication and computer skills needs of the students or other such skill needs that students could have.

A decision was taken that the quality study should leave out the goals altogether, especially as they were centrally given and not changeable at the time.

It was obvious to the group that the quality of higher education could not be measured in the classical way by productivity measurements like the number of credits or exams produced matched with the resources supplied. There were several disappointing examples of this type of study from the previous decade. One reason for their failure was that they did not measure the *quality* of the activities. But even as productivity measurements, those studies were poor because they did not pay attention to the specific items involved. A 'student' is not a constant. Students have very different experiences and can be selected in different ways, ·thus affecting the outcome of a given input. The same is true of teachers, not to mention the teachers' ambitions in fulfilling the somewhat vague official goals. A high ambition in one sense could produce a low number of exam passes and thus a low productivity. A high ambition in another sense could have an opposite consequence. Moreover, the productivity studies did not involve the customers of the system at all. This meant that the effectiveness of the system – defined in terms of the degree to which customers' needs and desires were satisfied – could not be judged.

For this study, therefore, a different evaluative model was developed. It concentrated on the *process*. It was an attempt to combine old-fashioned productivity models with more modern process thinking. It still employed much information on the resources entering the system and on the outcomes of the system but the main focus was on the processes. The columns of the resulting matrix were precisely the three groups of factors indicated: resources, process and outcome. The rows were organized according to the three main actors: the students, the teachers and the administration. Table 7.1 illustrates this and also gives some concrete examples of dimensions researched within each cell.

The self-evaluation inputs

For the self-evaluation part of the study a BA programme was chosen. The student population was about 280 at the Gothenburg School of Economics and about 800 all together for the four schools in the study.

The structural information was mainly gathered from secondary sources. Information on the students' part in the process was collected by survey. The inquiry was carried out at same time in all four schools and was analysed in one place. The teachers were also surveyed by a questionnaire. However, here each school analysed the results individually so comparisons were not as straightforward.

Information on organizational premises, on the administration and on the support activities involved were clarified by interviews with leaders and administrators in the system and also through secondary data gathering. Many results were taken from the records of exams

Table 7.1 *Evaluative pilot model of higher education, with examples*

Actors	Structure	Process	Results
Students	Admission competence	Time use on different programmes	Average study length for the exam
	Expectations	Time use on different self-activities	Drop-outs
	Financial and work conditions		Quality of exam results
Teachers	Competence	Overall planning of the courses	Course evaluations
	Expectations		Employers' evaluation
	Working and reward conditions	Teaching methods	Teachers' satisfaction
		Research findings integrated	
Administration/ support	Competence and philosophy	Strategies and organization	General image
	Financial strength of the organization	Staff development	Attractiveness to students and staff
			Costs per exam

and tests, exam papers, course evaluations, economic reports, staff turnover figures, publication records and so on.

The self-evaluation outcomes

Each school delivered a substantial report (Westlund, 1991) plus vast documentation consisting of exam papers, literature lists and so on. The findings were in different dimensions and measured along different scales. Some of the results were rather alarming. For instance the Gothenburg School of Economics found that the workload for students was too light at the basic level. It was also found that teachers were highly unsatisfied with the inadequate support system and with a lack of staff policy. On the other hand they liked student contact very much.

The self-evaluation made a SWOT analysis possible: strengths and weaknesses, opportunities and threats could be identified. This prompted more strategic discussions.

On another and lower level the results gave many detailed hints about possible changes in the operating system and in the pedagogical approach. Moreover, the external experts used the report as a basis for their audit and hearings and thus for their recommendations.

The external audit

The external experts were nominated by the task group and the final choice of the individuals was made by UHÄ. One was a professor in accounting and a former dean of the Bergen School of Economics, Norway, and the other was a former docent at the Stockholm School of Economics. Their audit was based partly upon the self-evaluation report and partly upon results from visits to the different schools which included hearings with the administration, a group of teachers, a group of students and some industry representatives.

Their report (Kinserdal and Ströberg, 1991) was composed of two different parts, one part with conclusions and overall comments on business administration courses and one part dealing with the separate schools. On the more general level the recommendations were for them to become more international, to stay with the present theoretical ambitions and to pay more attention to the pedagogics. The report also supported the idea of resource allocation according to results rather than by the number of students – a reform that was already on its way and has been implemented from 1 July 1993.

On the local level the Gothenberg School was the subject of some well-founded recommendations, namely to focus on chosen areas of excellence, to continue to build international networks, to involve the professors more in the basic courses and so on.

Shortcomings of the study

During information gathering it had been realized that the evaluative model was lacking a third dimension. The existence of an approach to a certain process was always registered and appraised according to the model, whereas the question of whether that approach was deployed and whether the results of the process were to be followed up were neglected. Thus whether a quality improvement loop was built into the system or not was not recorded. This was particularly obvious for the support systems. There was often said to be an adequate *approach* but in many cases quality was not actually achieved because there was no feedback and so implementation gaps appeared.

Another shortcoming was the fact that the study was not marketed effectively to leaders or staff of the chosen departments. This was partly due to the way in which the study was initiated and partly because too little interest was taken in these kinds of questions at the time. Because of these presentational and cultural factors the study has not yet led to many changes in the BA education.

Next round of quality evaluation

At the top level of the university, work has continued using total quality management (TQM) influenced ideas and systems aimed at securing continuous quality improvement. The board of the School of Economics has started working in the same direction.

The original multi-school task group has survived and is planning the next study. Acknowledging the main weakness from the first round it has been suggested that one of the available TQM evaluation models should replace the previously used model. The most obvious one to adopt in a Swedish study would be the Swedish Quality Award model produced by SIQ, the Swedish Institute for Quality Development, and similar to the Malcolm Baldrige model (SIQ, 1993).

The difference from the original model is first of all that the SIQ model maintains a clear distinction between quality evaluation and quality management. The pilot study did not make that distinction. According to the TQM approach it is necessary for quality management to have a continuous and close knowledge of the needs and desires of different customer groups, both internal and external. Therefore the evaluation procedure should register the existence or non-existence of systematically repeated surveys and inquiries. The field research that was carried out last time should therefore not be included this time. If the organization is TQM managed it should in any case be able to show such survey results over time.

Another change is the fact that the goal structure has to be considered. There are no longer any central directives other than on a very general level, and therefore there is every reason to focus on how the customer needs are converted into goals for every process, and what the degree of goal fulfilment is. The existence of quality feedback loops will also be looked for.

Finally the SIQ model also questions how the organization relates to its suppliers. For a university these could be anyone from editors to software manufacturers to the scientific society which delivers the teachers.

When the first evaluative round was carried out there was a clear reluctance on the part of the different schools concerning comparisons of assessments. The mere suggestion was upsetting to some people within the organizations. Slowly this has changed, and the decision now is to use the grading system that came from the model. The weight that is given in the basic model to the different criteria might be changed but the main intention of facilitating comparison between schools and over time will remain. Following the normal procedure when applying the SIQ model, external auditors will be used.

This has been, therefore, a story of change. Techniques have been sharpened, concepts have been clarified and attitudes have begun to shift. These organizations are learning to learn.

8

Costing Non-Conformance at an NHS Hospital: a Pilot Study

Richard Joss

Background

The large acute hospital in this study is located within a health authority that for the last eight years has been working towards implementing a quality management framework. This framework has rapidly moved from a general management development approach to one explicitly based on quality improvement. Although the term 'total quality management' (TQM) is not used by the health authority to describe its quality improvement activities, staff frequently refer to TQM when discussing their approach.

The basis for this cost of quality study, however, was the work of Crosby (1979). It was Crosby who suggested that the first step in any quality improvement programme should be an attempt to cost non-conformance. The purpose of this is twofold. The first is obviously to pinpoint where the major problems are occurring before taking corrective action. The second is to prove to senior management that the costs involved in systematic quality improvement activities can be recouped through reductions in error and waste.

Naturally most work on the cost of quality has been carried out in manufacturing organizations, and it is only in recent years that attention has moved to the commercial service sector. Relatively little work has been carried out on systematically identifying the cost of non-conformance in public sector health services. It is an area that has proved to be particularly sensitive, given constant pressure on resources and sporadic drives for cost improvement exercises in the UK's National Health Service (NHS).

The main focus of TQM experiments in the NHS continues to be on service improvement rather than attempts to reduce costs. Approaches have typically involved focusing on measuring patient satisfaction, providing better information to patients and carers and improving amenities (Joss et al., 1992). The study reported here is one of the few attempts to provide a detailed demonstration of the feasibility of identifying errors and waste in the NHS.

Although one normally associates costs of quality with reduction of errors and waste, strictly speaking the cost of quality is the sum of two separate costs. The first is the cost of non-conformance (error and waste), and the second is the cost of ensuring conformance (that is the costs involved in appraising and preventing non-conformance).

In all, therefore, there are held to be four types of costs:

Appraisal costs associated with quality control, for example through inspection and audit.

Prevention costs entailed in designing conformance into processes, that is quality assurance.

Internal failure costs arising from direct and indirect costs of errors and waste. They include both direct and indirect costs, for example redoing work or carrying extra stocks.

External failure costs associated with making good additional liabilities and responsibilities to the end user, for example litigation.

This study was principally aimed at identifying the internal failure costs associated with the running of a ward.

Summary of methods and measures

The cost of quality project took place on a 17-bed medicine for the elderly ward. It was carried out by a small project team involving administrators, nurse managers, and staff from the ward. They started by identifying all the main departments with which the ward had dealings. Thirteen departments were identified and they were surveyed about their perceptions of the services provided; the difficulties encountered in maintaining the service; and the potential for improvement.

The project team brainstormed the problems encountered on the ward when dealing with these other departments. This produced a list of some 30 issues that affected the provision of 'a quality service' to patients at each stage of the process from admission to discharge. A short study was also carried out of activity on the ward to provide further information about working patterns, time spent on particular tasks and the problems that arose in day-to-day activity. Checklists were then developed to collect data on potential areas of non-conformance. These were filled in by ward staff using a sample of patients arriving on the ward over a two-week period.

Results of the problem analysis stage

Eleven general areas were identified where problems had occurred and which had resulted in errors or waste. They are described below but, for reasons that will become apparent, only seven were subsequently used to identify the cost of non-conformance.

Several assumptions were made about the costs of running the ward. Where errors or waste resulted in one or more full *bed days* being lost, then the cost of a bed day was used. Where the costs incurred were of the order of hours rather than days, then staff costs were used. Where it was not possible to use either of these measures, the team merely 'noted the number of patients affected by the problems'.

Running costs for the ward were calculated as follows. The ward had 17 beds that theoretically provided 6205 bed days per year. On average the ward admitted 250 patients per year, making an average stay of 25 days. The hospital costs a patient bed day at approximately £74, giving a patient bed cost of £459,170 per year. The direct costs of staffing the ward over a 24-hour period were calculated at about £350 per day or £127,655 per year. This figure does not include sickness, annual leave, maternity leave or study leave. The problem areas and cost calculations are as follows.

Ambulance waiting time

Undue delays in collecting patients and bringing them in for treatment were found to affect 62 patients per year or 25 per cent of total admissions. This resulted in delays to the start of treatment and was also distressing to the patients. It was clearly an internal failure cost for the ambulance service but it was difficult to calculate the impact on the actual running of the ward, and this area remained uncosted.

Delays in admitting patients on the ward

The primary problem here was over-stretched staff who were struggling to cope with patients who had already been admitted. Most delays were found to be small, but approximately one patient per week (20 per cent of all patients) was subjected to substantial delay. There were some associated direct costs. For example, if delays meant that the patient was not admitted until after 6.00 p.m. then any tests called for required a taxi to transport specimens to the laboratory for testing. Laboratory staff also had to be called out. These costs would affect the laboratories' budgets but, since there was no cross-charging at the time of the study, the wards did not have to bear these additional costs. There were also associated indirect costs. For example late admissions would be handled by the doctor on call. This meant that the senior house officer would have to repeat the exercise merely to get to know the patient the following day. Again, these costs were not quantified.

Discrepancies of information
Poor or incomplete paperwork at the point of admission was calculated to cost 26 hours a year of senior staff time (£156). This does not include other time wasted on ward administration (see below).

Wasted time in general ward administration
This was time unnecessarily spent by the ward clerk chasing up problems with other departments including X-ray, works' department and laundry. The figure amounted to 104 hours per year or two full working weeks, although the money concerned was only £260.

Delays in receiving pathology results
This proved to be a major cost area. It was calculated that delays amounted, in all, to one day per week. On the assumption that this resulted in 52 lost bed days per year, the figure would be £3,848. This would only be a rough estimate since it would not always be the case that waiting for a day for results would mean a patient actually having to stay an extra day in hospital. However, it does suggest the general order of costs. Furthermore, analysis of the reasons showed substantial problems in administering the process. For example 15–20 per cent of the specimens sent for testing had to be returned because of wrong labelling, illegible handwriting, no doctor's signature, or no address for the results to be sent to. In some 5 per cent of the cases, specimens were so badly damaged that they could not be tested and had to be retaken. Again, this would distress patients, but the additional costs would still not be borne by the ward. Of course, when full ward budgeting is in place including the costs of support services, then these figures will be a major consideration.

Waiting times for patients in X-ray
It was difficult to cost this item since there was no agreed basis for costing acceptable waiting time with the X-ray department. However, occasionally nurses had to accompany patients to X-ray and could be away for over two hours, thus reducing ward cover.

Lost and delayed X-rays
The radiology department did not keep figures on lost X-rays, or the number of X-rays that had to be redone. However, this pilot study calculated that the time spent waiting for repeat X-rays to be organized and carried out amounted to 78 bed days per year. Again, assuming that some patients had to stay in an extra day because of this, the costs would amount to £5,772 per year.

Infections and pressure sores
Here the study was on safer ground in that a more accurate estimate could be made of lost days. Chest infections and pressure sores were calculated to extend the inpatient stays of 12 people per year for an average of nine days. These extra bed days cost £7,992 per year. These costs do not include additional expenditure on costs of drugs, dressing and so on.

Complaints
Complaints were seen to be an external failure cost and were not addressed within this study, although they are obviously very important dimensions of quality.

Injuries at work
Lifting injuries proved to be a major cost consideration. Five members of staff per year were injured in lifting accidents and took a total of 205 days sick leave. This resulted in costs of £3,600 for wages while they were off sick.

Discharges delayed through placement problems
Approximately 48 patients per year were found to experience delays on discharge. Total days lost amounted to 480 days per year or £35,520. This was a major issue involving several different agencies including the social services, and has since become a priority area for corrective action.

Internal costs summary
The five areas involving the highest direct internal failure costs are shown in Figure 8.1. The total (£56,732) provides a rough guide to the internal failure costs to the ward concerned. However, it does not include the internal failure costs of other departments – for example X-ray and pathology. It is interesting to note that these figures alone reflect some 10–12 per cent of the total running costs of the ward and are within the general parameters of recoverable costs claimed by Crosby (1979) and Atkinson (1990).

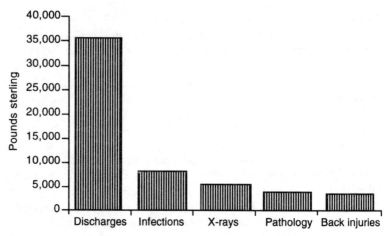

Figure 8.1   *Internal failure costs on a medicine for the elderly ward*

Discussion

This was a limited, but nevertheless important, pilot study carried out in the face of some scepticism, not to say opposition, from medical and finance staff. In particular, equating days lost from delayed X-rays or pathology tests with bed days lost was found to be only a crude approximation. The finance department also pointed out that any savings made could only be invested in greater patient throughput. Since 'the money did not actually follow the patient', this would perversely result in increased costs in laundry, drugs and so on. The hospital was not yet at the stage where greater throughput would result in greater income, although increased efficiency might later help to secure future contracts with purchasers.

The study resulted in the setting up of quality improvement groups to look more closely at particular areas of the findings. These included groups on X-ray, discharge and pressure sores. A 'cost of quality' pack was designed to help other departments to carry out their own studies and a more elaborate exercise is now under way in the hospital. It is not yet clear what savings will result from these studies, although it is almost certain that substantial gains will be made by improving discharge arrangements.

The major gain, however, proved to be the raising of staff awareness of the issue of non-conformance. Previously it was generally thought that few, if any, savings could be made in costs. Typically, government calls for cost savings of as little as 1 per cent resulted in reductions in staff numbers or freezing of recruitment, rather than concerted effort to reduce waste. This study points to the major savings that are possible without the automatic need to reduce staff resources.

Broader issues

One weakness with the approach taken was that it focused primarily on efficiency rather than effectiveness. Thus, where a process was not seen to produce errors or waste, it could remain unchallenged. However, there might be alternative ways of doing things which might produce improvements in processes that were already thought to be operating well. One might also ask the question, 'Should the patient have been admitted in the first place?' The reliability and validity of medical decisions to admit patients were not analysed or costed, nor was the value or otherwise of different tests and procedures that were carried out once patients had been admitted.

Problem of operational definitions

For something to be judged an error, for example under the Crosby approach, one must define the acceptable parameters. For instance one might decide that a 20-minute wait for an X-ray was acceptable. In this case errors would therefore only occur outside this limit. As Deming (1986) has argued, substantial improvements might be made by a better understanding of the statistical variations in aggregated examples, both within and outside such arbitrary standards. This would lead to a stronger identification with the TQM idea of continuous improvement.

Costs of healthy communities

Beyond the scope of this study, but of key importance to quality improvement, would be the development of models for costing the provision of health care to communities *as a whole*. For example, rapid treatment of more acute cases (such as coronaries and strokes) would push up the costs to the hospital concerned, but might well considerably reduce the costs of expensive maintenance of patients in the community whilst they were awaiting surgery. Current applications of TQM approaches are nowhere near providing costing models for tracking these macro issues.

Involvement of the consumer

A major weakness of the approaches taken to costing non-conformance, as used in this study, is the lack of involvement of patients, carers and other external stakeholders. Costs were calculated using professionally derived criteria which were designed, implemented and interpreted by professional staff. Costs were limited to direct financial costs and did not consider the pain and distress caused to patients by the need to take additional blood samples or to spend extra days in hospital because of unnecessary chest infections or pressure sores. Of course, costing pain and distress is problematic, not least because it invites payment of compensation. But it can be done: insurance companies have been paying out for pain and distress for years.

To ignore this aspect because it is difficult to measure may lead to a quality improvement programme playing down, or denying the relevance of, a patient's perceptions to the costing of non-conformance. It would be quite possible to end up with an efficient, costed and well-managed service which no one wants or which has no demonstrated benefits. Given that implementation of TQM and the resulting models of costing non-conformance can have dramatic results, and possibly unintended and unwanted side effects, there is an urgent need for more research in the whole area of identifying and measuring the cost of quality.

Note

The study on which this chapter is based was undertaken by Sue Damarell-Kewell from the health authority concerned. Permission to cite her data is gratefully acknowledged.

9

Quality Improvement in the Dutch Department of Defence

Nico Mol

This case study focuses on the attempts at quality improvement in the Dutch Department of Defence. These attempts are embodied in projects aiming at 'integral care for quality' (in Dutch *Integrale Kwaliteitszorg*), started at the end of the 1980s in several units of the department. One of these projects specifically will be the object of our inquiry: the quality improvement project implemented in the National Logistic Command (NLC), the organization unit responsible for general logistic support and maintenance of material equipment on behalf of the Dutch land forces. This project is considered to be the most advanced and successful one in this area in the department. Experiences obtained in NLC are hoped to provide a base for similar innovations in other units of the defence organization.

Like government in general and defence in particular, NLC has been subjected in recent years to severe budget cuts, in its case accompanied by fairly radical reorganizations. Performance thereby has been under close scrutiny, not only stemming from the quest for 'lean government' and the realization of 'peace dividends', but from doubts about NLC's performance as well. Many tasks of NLC being of the business type, comparisons with private sector activities could be made rather easily and from these comparisons unfavourable judgements often did result.

To meet the double challenge implied – that is, to adjust to the reductions in the means available and to improve the quality of its services at the same time – NLC adopted in the late 1980s a management system called 'quality management by quality objectives' (QMbO). A key element in the adoption of this system was the intention to fulfil ISO certification requirements for NLC units. The ideas underlying QMbO thereby reflected in many ways the Allied Quality Assurance Publications (AQAP) standards traditionally applied by NATO countries to private suppliers of defence material. Thus, the application of similar performance requirements to NLC might prove NLC's competitiveness even in the absence of any actual competition (and of course all the more so with respect to activities under threat of being contracted out to private firms, such as various maintenance services).

Accordingly, the quality concept constituting the point of departure for the QMbO system was derived from its NEN-ISO definition, published by the Netherlands Normalization Institute:

> the whole of the attributes and characteristics of a product or service relevant to the fulfilment of stated or evident needs.

This quality concept was especially favoured because it stressed the desirability to express quality objectives in explicit and measurable criteria, thus enhancing objectivity in the evaluation of performance.

For the implementation of the concept of so-called TAPROs (task programmes), defining performance indicators and setting standards for them, were to be designed. These TAPROs then should become the instruments to guide the activities of NLC and its subunits. Within NLC, specifically 750 and 785 maintenance commands (a regional unit for general maintenance and a central unit for maintenance of electronic equipment, respectively) would be leading in the development of the TAPROs intended in the QMbO system. First drafts of these TAPROs were submitted for 1991: improved updates have been presented since (the design of 1994 TAPROs was under scrutiny at the end of 1993).

After a brief description of QMbO (as documented in spring 1990) and the structure of the TAPROs derived from it (documented in autumn 1991), empirical findings with respect to the TAPROs involved will be presented. Subsequently, these finding will be analysed and evaluated. Attention will be focused on the question to what extent definite conclusions about the quality of NLC's services may be inferred from the indicators provided by the TAPRO reports. Thereby some obstacles to performance evaluation based on these TAPROs will be discussed. Finally it will be noted that QMbO has not been applied in full accordance with original intentions and that possibilities for quality improvement by QMbO are ultimately limited by the quality concept underlying this management system.

Outline of QMbO

The ideas underlying QMbO have their origin in the general striving towards decentralization of management control in Dutch government organizations, generally labelled as 'self-management'. Self-management thereby was defined as 'an internal decentralization of responsibilities and competences to lower levels of management'. In QMbO this decentralization was intended to be accompanied by integral care for quality, to guarantee adequate service levels in the self-managing units. Thus, QMbO was supposed to blend together the concepts of 'management by exception' and 'management by objectives' in management control by NLC.

Quality objectives, to be identified in the application of QMbO, should be expressed in measurable targets to be realized within definite time limits. Upon those targets, task programmes – TAPROs – could then be based, to be agreed upon by NLC and its organization units. Such an agreement would imply a bilateral commitment from these units and from the central command of NLC respectively. The units of NLC would commit themselves to the fulfilment of the tasks specified, while NLC in turn would provide them with the means and the competences necessary to accomplish these tasks.

In developing these ideas of QMbO a design of the general structure of the TAPROs was arrived at during 1991. According to this design, the task programmes should be based on a strategic plan. This plan would encompass an analysis of strengths/weaknesses and opportunities/threats from which long-run objectives for the organization unit should be derived. Subsequently, short-run objectives stated in measurable targets were to be deduced as yearly task programmes for the unit, afterwards to be compared with actual outcomes. Thus, the TAPROs should be presented in the following format:

1 strategic plan;
2 task programme and evaluation of outcomes;
3 means and competences.

A two-step procedure was developed to draft the task programmes. First, the activities of the organization unit should be clustered in so-called functional areas, and within these areas 'priority result areas' should be identified. Secondly, for those priority result areas performance indicators should be chosen, and target values for those indicators set.

According to this format and procedure then, TAPROs have been structured for 750 and 785 maintenance commands and for NLC as a whole. With some alterations this format has served TAPRO planning and reporting from 1991 onwards.

Results

In our presentation of empirical findings with respect to the actual implementation of the TAPROs, we will focus on the task

Table 9.1   *Specifications in the task programmes, 1993*

	Functional areas	Priority result areas	Performance indicators
750	12	40	60
785	10	27	40
NLC	11	14	16

programmes in which the (measurable) targets are being specified. In all task programmes investigated – for 750, 785 and NLC – the indented procedure has been clearly distinguishable. Thus, for each of these programmes functional areas are listed, priority result areas identified, performance indicators specified and targets for these indicators determined. In the task programmes for 1993 the areas and indicators for the respective organization units are shown in Table 9.1.

In all task programmes the functional areas may be classified into areas belonging to primary processes and areas related to secondary processes of the organization. Areas with respect to primary processes cover all maintenance activities. Areas for secondary processes encompass activities like 'quality management' and 'organization and information' intended to support NLC's services to its clients indirectly. Performance measurement has been following fundamentally different approaches in those two classes.

Indicators with respect to primary processes have all been quantified to allow for some kind of overall evaluation of performance in those processes. The indicators related to maintenance of vehicles or equipment usually specify percentages of time overruns in delivery or projects finished, and so on. For those indicators precise target values are being stated, so in the TAPRO evaluation reports definite judgements can be made about their realization.

With respect to secondary processes, however, indicators cannot be related to characteristics of performance in those processes at all. The indicators listed in the task programmes rather represent targets set on plans or policies on behalf of management of the organization units. Typically we may encounter indicators like 'plan for area X determined' or 'policy for area Y adopted', just specifying the availability of documents in which these plans or policies are elaborated. Targets thereby imply no more than deadlines for this availability. However, for the purpose of this case study we may limit

Table 9.2   *Specification of primary processes in task programmes, 1993*

	Functional areas	Product type	Performance indicators
750	1	8	20
785	1	6	18
NLC	4	6	8

Table 9.3   *Performance indicators in task programmes, 1993*

	Input indicators	Output indicators	Effect indicators
750	8		12
785	6	6	6
NLC		1	7

our investigation to the primary processes involved. Performance measurement for these processes should reflect the quality of services NLC actually provides to its consumers. In the analysis to be presented here, the functional areas related to secondary processes therefore will be ignored.

Eliminating secondary processes from Table 9.1, the remaining specifications of functional areas, priority result areas (for primary processes to be conceived as types of products) and performance indicators are shown in Table 9.2. The indicators in the last column will now be analysed in more detail.

Analysis

In examining the empirical findings in the TAPROs for 1993, we will first analyse to what extent the performance of NLC is being reflected in the indicators chosen. Next, we will try to evaluate the impact that performance measurement may have on the quality of NLC's services.

With respect to the objects measured, the performance indicators presented in the TAPROs may be placed into three categories: (1) inputs used, (2) outputs obtained and (3) results or effects achieved by the activities performed. In Table 9.3 the distribution of the indicators over these three categories is presented.

In QMbO this categorization may be interpreted as a ranking of the three types of indicator with respect to their proximity to the quality concept underlying the system. Only results achieved, measured by effect indicators, can be related immediately to this concept, already defined above as 'the fulfilment of stated or evident needs'. Output and input variables as such do not represent valid indicators for 'quality' thus defined.

From the point of view of QMbO, then, the majority of the indicators actually do reflect quality. Further inspection of these effect indicators reveals that they themselves can be grouped into three types:

1 indicators measuring 'readiness for use', calculated as a percentage of vehicles or equipment used by clients served (operational units of the Dutch land forces);
2 indicators measuring 'requests fulfilled', calculated as a percentage of requests from clients served for supplies from NLC's stocks;
3 indicators measuring 'in-time delivery', calculated as a percentage of maintenance projects executed on behalf of NLC's clients.

In the TAPROs explicit target percentages have been stated for each indicator, to be compared with actual percentages reported afterwards.

However, obstacles to performance measurement soon posed themselves. In a number of cases questions have been raised with respect to the precise definitions of the indicators to be used. For example, the calculation of a percentage for the indicator 'requests fulfilled' could be based either upon requests actually submitted or upon requests authorized only (outcomes for some years thereby leading to opposite conclusions about performance). In other cases data bases proved to be incomplete or data processing systems not yet operational to give the information required.

At the end of 1993, most of these obstacles seemed to have been surmounted. Thus, adequate reporting on performance is supposed to have become effective in 1994. In TAPROs for 1994, therefore, precise and detailed requirements with respect to the information to be provided have been specified. As yet, no general conclusions about performance can be drawn from TAPRO evaluation reports thus far presented. Evaluations have been limited to listings of targets realized and targets not realized (in the latter case followed by some comments on possible causes), whenever the information available allowed such a listing to be made.

The evaluation of QMbO in this case study therefore will not be based on actual outcomes of performance measurement in NLC or its subunits. Instead, we will focus upon the impact of the system as perceived by concerned members of the NLC organization and the Dutch land forces. Thereby we will comment on some deficiencies to be inferred from the analysis presented above.

Evaluation

As has been stated, the quality improvement project developed and implemented in NLC is generally regarded as a success. NLC's TAPRO system may be judged to exemplify the striving towards efficiency and effectiveness in the whole of the Defence Department. Thus, many other organization units in the department are trying to set up indicator systems modelled on the performance measurement in NLC's task programmes.

Nevertheless, it has to be acknowledged that no empirical evidence can be produced to give these favourable perceptions an objective foundation. Two related developments in the Department of Defence may be recognized as inhibiting any unambiguous evaluation of the impact of the TAPRO system on NLC's performance.

First, NLC has been subjected during the whole period of QMbO's implementation to rigorous reorganizations. From the end of the 1980s onwards two reorganization projects have been put into effect. The present 750 and 785 maintenance commands as such were created in 1992. By the end of 1993 already a third reorganization was under way, implying a fusion of NLC with several other organization units into one so-called National Command (NATCO).

The second – related – reason pertains to the general reduction of the Dutch land forces, implying a continuous decrease in workloads for NLC during the whole period of QMbO. While levels of production are declining, excess capacity can result in higher percentages for the effect indicators calculated.

The instability of the setting in which QMbO has been introduced may explain why the intended management system has not yet become fully effective. The development of the task programmes analysed above has not been accompanied by any substantial decentralization of responsibilities and competences, to realize the 'management by exception' and 'management by objectives' ideas underlying the system. Obviously, then, performance measurement incorporated in the task programmes has not as yet really been put to the test. No real weight has been loaded on the indicators chosen as a foundation for the QMbO management system. So the question remains to what extent the indicator system developed actually might underpin quality judgements, whenever NLC's environment has been sufficiently stabilized for QMbO's full implementation.

Examination of the effect indicators presented in the task programmes will clarify that 'quality as intended' (according to QMbO's quality concept) is only partially represented by them. Goal achievement as measured by these indicators cannot be identified unambiguously with realization of adequate quality levels in NLC's activities.

Specifically, three deficiencies in performance measurement may be noted here. First, measurement may be biased by heterogeneity of the vehicles, equipment or projects contained in the numbers counted for these respective entities. Usually, units measured will show a wide variety of characteristics which might be considered relevant in any comparison of planned and actual numbers. Generally, those characteristics will not be identically distributed in the sums of vehicles, equipment or projects targeted and calculated. Outcomes thus will be inevitably misleading to some extent. Furthermore, clearly, indicator values might be biased. Priorities in executing projects could be adjusted to reach targets set for in-time delivery percentages; readiness for use percentages might be attained by postponing complicated repairs; and so on.

Secondly, measurement may be incomplete because not all of NLC's services will be identified as vehicles or equipment processed or as projects executed. Actual service levels will be represented only partially by the indicator values, additional assistance by NLC being provided as a free service. Again a tendency may exist to misrepresent actual performance, for example by transforming free services into projects for bookkeeping purposes only.

Thirdly, the indicators are aiming at some aspect of quality (being ready for use or delivered in time) and do not legitimize any overall judgement with respect to quality as such. Vehicles or equipment may be included as ready for use, even when problems encountered have been solved only temporarily; good may be counted as delivered in time even when requests have not been met according to initial specifications; and so on.

Thus, whenever evaluation of performance focuses on particular indicators, organizational units may resort to window dressing to comply with the objectives specified for them. Obviously, then, the figures presented should be handled with care in such an evaluation of NLC's activities. This is especially so because the effect indicators calculated are not embedded in a more comprehensive framework,

allowing a systematic analysis of their variances. NLC's cost accounting system for instance does not have the capability to relate costs
incurred to them. The TAPRO system does not provide the
information required for an operational audit, in which unambiguous
judgements could be made of the levels of efficiency and effectiveness
implied by the indicators measured.

Conclusions

Obviously, the scope for applying the indicator system developed in
the TAPROs to an evaluation of the quality of NLC's services is
limited. Many refinements would be necessary for definite judgements about the quality of those services to be derived. But with all
the efforts already spend in implementing this management system,
which elaborations would be sufficient to realize this objective in the
future?

However, such a strategy, just aiming at a further expansion of the
indicator systems in the task programmes, may not even be desirable.
Two reasons may be given for amending NLC's present approach to
quality improvement more fundamentally, as follows.

Ambiguity in the task programmes
In line with the strictly hierarchical structure of military organizations, the TAPROs are oriented at an agreement between the
commanding officers of the organization units and their superiors.
These agreements are only partly directed at performance of the
organization units as such. To a large extent the agreements focus on
the way the units should be managed internally. Thereby the
agreements do not in fact reflect the concept of 'management by
objectives' – the substitution of input by output controls – as was
intended. Rather they try to provide explicit guidance with respect to
internal management control, to reduce the need for *ad hoc*
interventions by superiors.

The number and nature of the indicators developed for NLC's
secondary processes may illuminate this point. As may be clear from
the empirical findings presented above, performance indicators for
NLC's services as such are outnumbered by indicators related to
plans or policies. Characteristically the entities measured are documents, having as their main purpose to provide management with
monitoring opportunities.

Thus, the intention of 'management by exception' has been given some substance in the TAPROs, but the quasi-objectives of 'documents to be available' cannot be considered to express QMbO's underlying idea of MbO.

Deficiency of the quality concept
The quality concept of QMbO stresses the objective measurability of quality characteristics. Thereby, indicator values may be calculated from NLC's own information systems (when these systems will be fully operative). Needs and judgements of NLC's immediate clients – the operational units dependent on NLC for logistic support – will be expressed only indirectly in these calculations. The evaluation of performance focuses on deviance from targets for which these needs and judgements are not decisive. So, quality evaluation tends to become an inwardly focused activity for NLC.

As a consequence, this approach to performance evaluation may reduce NLC's sensitivity to its 'markets'. To keep NLC competitive, perceptions of the quality of its services will be relevant.

Recommendations
In our view, then, two amendments to the TAPRO system as developed in NLC would be desirable. First, performance measurement should be tuned systematically to the realization of 'management by objectives' originally intended in QMbO. Task programmes should be directed at characteristics of NLC's services exclusively. Directives with respect to internal management (regarding documents to be produced, and so on) should be integrated eventually – such bureaucratic devices to be avoided as much as possible – in the agreements on delegated competences accompanying those programmes in the TAPROs.

Secondly, for service centres like NLC quality improvement should start from the needs of their immediate consumers. Task programmes determined by superiors should at least be supplemented by contracts agreed upon with the clients themselves. These would help to guide the design of a quality control system for those centres.

Ultimately, QMbO as such may be especially appropriate for mission centres in the military organization, where priorities are set centrally and explicitly. For operational units in military organizations the NLC's laborious development of new management systems may hold useful lessons.

10

Enhancing Quality in the Police Service: Leicestershire Constabulary

Stephen Hanney

The 1990 *Operational Policing Review* (Joint Consultative Committee) was not the start of the pursuit of quality in the police service within the UK but it was a significant milestone. It gave an impetus to the police consideration of quality which incorporated, and in some cases preceded, the general thrust towards paying greater attention to quality, particularly as perceived by customers, within the public services. This chapter briefly analyses some of the moves towards enhancing quality within the British police services before focusing on developments within Leicestershire Constabulary, two of whose chief officers played a major role in the national debate.

Following the doubts raised in the *Operational Policing Review* about public confidence in the police and in the developing style of policing, the Association of Chief Police Officers (ACPO) established a Working Party whose 1990 report, *Setting the Standards for Policing: Meeting Community Expectation* was

> intended to provide a corporate statement of values for the police Forces of England and Wales, a strategic framework to identify and improve the quality of service delivery and a system to monitor and measure over time Police Service ability to meet public expectations and consequently increase public confidence in it. (para. 4)

As noted in *Considering Quality* (CEPPP, 1992: para. 178) there is a relatively strong tradition of public opinion surveys derived, in part, 'from the principle that British policing is based upon public consent'. Many such surveys have been conducted since the early 1980s (see e.g. Jones and Levi, 1983). The importance of policing by consent was stressed by the Chairman of the ACPO Working Party and Chief Constable of Leicestershire Constabulary, Michael Hirst, who also chaired the ACPO Quality of Service Committee responsible for the 'quality initiative'. He observed that the public has neither freedom of choice in who provides the policing service, nor the ability to provide sanctions for poor service delivery. Therefore, he claimed, in policing, meeting public expectation and achieving public satisfaction have to be among the service's key performance measures. For the same reasons it is imperative that quality dimensions of policing are agreed with the public and the measurements open to scrutiny. Policing by consent is a phrase we have used for many years but we are only now beginning to appreciate its full implications. (Hirst, 1991: 184)

The then Deputy Chief Constable of Leicestershire, Tony Butler, also emphasized how, in the move in the 1990s towards debating quality, the definition has given primacy to the expectations or needs of customers. He stated:

the title of the document *Setting the Standards for Policing: Meeting Community Expectations* demonstrates the extent to which the document understands the meaning of the concept of quality. The extensive literature on the issue of quality of products or services points out that quality is relative and always relates to the expectations or needs of the customer. In fact, a commitment to delivering quality services demands the determination of what the customer expects and then responding accordingly. (Butler, 1992a: 26)

This police definition of quality as being related to customer expectations is an important example in the general move in this direction in British public services. This is recognized by a team from Brunel University which analysed various techniques for exploring the gap between the services expected by the public and those provided (Brunel University, 1993). However, such an approach is not the only one currently in use. The Audit Commission (1992) has concentrated on a much narrower concept of efficiency in a range of predefined areas which, contrary to the statement in the recent White Paper *Police Reform* (Cmnd 2218), are not necessarily those most related to public expectations (Home Office, 1993). The importance of this is that if police forces are encouraged to concentrate on areas that are not necessarily those of greatest concern to the public, the latter's satisfaction with the service might decline even though the force achieves a high efficiency rating. Similar fears were expressed in 1984 by Jones and Silverman.

The key to the ACPO quality initiative is not just that public opinion is surveyed, but that performance is measured against standards which reflect public expectations. Hirst claimed:

to begin to make any sense of the abstract concept of quality and to refine it into a measurable achievement, it has to be reduced to performance standards which, while meeting statutory requirements, also reflect public expectation. Only by measurement against predetermined standards will the quality dimension of service bear comparison with results, year on year, between forces and between service delivery units. (1991: 185)

The setting of standards raises serious and complex questions about the potential clash between producer preferences (those of either the local force or the Home Office) and customer preferences. The police may also believe that it would not be operationally effective to devote the level of resources to preferences apparently desired by the public such as a massive increase in levels of foot patrolling. In 1992 Butler revised his book, *Police Management*, to incorporate, 'the notion of meeting community expectations through the setting of standards of police services' (1992b: ix). In this he recognized that inevitably the setting of standards would involve compromises between community expectations, operational effectiveness and resource constraints:

> There may be a need to negotiate a compromise between the 'ideal' service, as identified by community expectations, and the 'possible' which can be achieved within the resource limitations. This will be a test of the sub-divisional commander's skill in consulting the community and marketing the service to customers. (p. 110)

A further aspect of this problem is that the various types of customer may each have a different perspective. This issue was discussed by Her Majesty's Inspectorate of Constabulary (HMIC, 1991) and the main, sometimes overlapping, categories identified included: victims, that is all those who have become victims and have called upon the services of the police for assistance; suspects; callers, included both personal and telephone callers seeking advice, assistance or information; participative users, that is positive voluntary users of the service including witnesses; and other users, that is the vast majority of the population who do not actively come into contact with the police but who nevertheless are indirectly affected by the quality of service provided within their community.

At the Quality of Service Seminar in December 1992 three sets of performance indicators (PIs) were launched (ACPO, 1992). Those from the ACPO Quality of Service Committee consisted entirely of the percentage satisfaction with different aspects of policing. For some questions, such as satisfaction with the perceived levels of foot and mobile patrols, the general public is to be surveyed, but other questions will be targeted more specifically at victims, users and, in the case of traffic violations, suspects. The other PI sets came from HMIC and the Audit Commission. The Audit Commission's indicators were part of its *Citizen's Charter* indicators (Audit Commission, 1992) and were more in line with the 1980s stress on efficiency and value for money emphasized in the Home Office Circular 114/83, *Manpower, Effectiveness and Efficiency* (see Home Office, 1983 and Carter et al., 1992). ACPO's quality initiative meant, however, that various forces were in a good position to respond to the *Citizen's Charter* and three forces – Kent, Dyfed Powys and South Yorkshire – were among the first organizations to be awarded the Charter Mark.

Much of the quality initiative within the police service, and the incorporation of aspects of the *Citizen's Charter* movement, are well illustrated by developments in Leicestershire. Leicestershire Constabulary's *Policing Charter* (1993) shows how the national quality initiative has been integrated into the *Charter*, and later in the year the force was given a Charter Mark in the second round of such awards. The aim of the Constabulary is described as being, 'to provide the highest quality of policing service for the people of Leicestershire, within the resources available'. The definition of highest quality is given as:

> Delivering services that meet community expectations
> – making the most effective use of our resources
> – giving the best value for money.

To improve quality a framework was adopted to set, monitor and evaluate performance in delivering services within five key service areas. The way the concept will be operationalized is described as follows: 'The expectations expressed by the public will influence a series of service delivery standards. These standards will be a guarantee of quality to the public and a commitment to provide a quality service by our staff.' These sentences in the 1993 *Charter* are very similar to the original goals of the quality initiative in Leicestershire Constabulary. These were stated in a report prepared for the Chief Constable's Meeting Community Expectations Seminar in 1991 (Leicestershire Constabulary, 1991):

1 To define public expectations for service delivery standards.
2 To agree service delivery standards within existing resources
3 To achieve a clarity of understanding amongst all staff of the need to, and the means of, meeting community expectations.
4 To improve efficiency of internal systems by compliance with quality standards.

The report described the initial findings of an 18-month study of standards, beginning in spring 1991, during which samples from various categories of customers, including victims and callers, were questioned and their opinions and perceptions set alongside those of police officers.

The example of burglary from houses will be used to illustrate the process. The sequence and number of visits/contacts by the police seemed to have evolved 'naturally' in response to a variety of pressures including the rising number of burglaries, which meant there were too few detectives to make the initial visits to all burglaries. Sub-divisional liaison officers identified up to 28 tasks that officers may have to complete in visiting the scene of a burglary, 'dependent on circumstances and largely subject to their own discretion'.

Liaison officers surveyed 26 victims of dwelling-house burglaries and found that those tasks which contributed directly to detection of offenders were readily recalled, whilst those which fell within the description of 'service' were, with the exception of being offered reassurance, recalled by only a very small number. The various tasks involved in the three visits most victims received (first officer at scene, second visit, scenes of crime officer (SOCO)) were identified and victims recalled receiving these to differing degrees. Comments gathered from officers conducting the various visits included some to the effect that the first officers to attend the scene felt they were not receiving sufficient information from their control rooms. The second officers attending the scene did not know what had happened prior to their arrival, and the scenes of crime officers would have liked closer liaison with investigating officers. With regard to police expectations the report concluded: 'There is evidence that there is a shortfall between the service provided by the force and that which it wishes to, and perceives that it does, supply. Internally, the needs to colleagues are either unknown or ignored.'

Although public satisfaction with the service was quite high, seven of the 26 rated it only as average and one as poor, and in each of these cases the report concluded that the service had 'failed to meet either the customers' needs or their expectations'. In the survey victims were asked what made them feel good or bad about the service they received, and it was found that there was a strong correlation between the two. If a particular service was provided or quality demonstrated, a good feeling was generated: if they were absent, a bad feeling was generated. This is shown in Table 10.1.

When asked what additional service they would have liked, victims replied: information of progress, detailed security advice, faster response. None of the victims felt that any part of the service provided was unnecessary. The report concluded:

Table 10.1   *Victims' opinions of police service*

Good feeling	Bad feeling
Promptness	Slow response (uniform, CID) No telephone contact.
Professionalism, efficiency	Failure to deliver promised service, causing unrealistic expectations
Good service from SOCO	Failure of SOCO to attend or long wait
Attitude of officers: caring reassuring	Some not as friendly as others
Being kept informed, revisit	Being left in lurch, no revisit
Detection	
Property recovered	
Crime prevention advice	

Source: Leicestershire Constabulary, 1991

> The survey indicates that the community expectations and needs are largely being met but there is a need in some cases for that little extra to provide a quality service. The main need appears to be for information after the crime, prompt service, crime prevention advice and guarantees of good caring and professional attitudes by officers. In terms of expectations there is a need to ensure they are not raised unjustifiably.

The issues raised by the survey include: the lack of both a standard model and consistency in service delivery; the need to guarantee response times; the need for effective monitoring, 'to ensure the service meets our own and the community's needs and which reflects realistic expectations'; 'officers' discretion over which services to provide need to be linked to service standards and public expectations'; 'the system needs to facilitate continual improvement of quality, both internally and externally.' The final point reflects some of the thinking of total quality management which was informing the process to some extent.

Having conducted the surveys a long process was required in each of the key service areas for which standards are to be set by Leicestershire Constabulary and performance monitored. The standards had to be developed, piloted and revised. In developing the standards use was made not only of local surveys but also of various Home Office Circulars, including 40/1992, and national research findings, including the *Victim's Charter* (Home Office, 1990) and *British Crime Surveys* (e.g. OPCS, 1993). This again raises the problem of how to reconcile the possibly conflicting demands. The initial piloting of the crime standards revealed not only that the standards were too elaborate, but also that there were great difficulties in attempting implementation without fully involving the workforce – especially middle managers – in a bottom-up way. The discretion of the lower ranks, similar to that of other 'street level bureaucrats' (Lipsky, 1980), and the powerful police front-line subculture, have been discussed by another of Leicestershire's officers working in this field (Brookes, 1991).

Following two stages of piloting it was recognized that it is necessary to ensure two things. First, as far as possible the process of implementation, especially the mechanisms for monitoring performance, should be owned by the workforce, and therefore acceptable to the police culture. Secondly, adequate training should be provided to supervisors.

The first standards to be introduced in Leicestershire Constabulary were not those for burglaries from dwellings, which are part of the 'management of crime' service area, but those in the area of the 'management of calls from the public'. Thus, following a similar process of surveying the callers, standards of service were set, piloted and eventually published for answering telephone calls. In this case benchmarks or baselines were published from existing management information. A leaflet issued in spring 1993, under the umbrella of the *Policing Charter*, was entitled 'Our standards of service: when you telephone us'. It sets out the various standards, including: 'If you ring 999 emergency you can expect your call to be answered within 15 seconds.' For each standard the benchmark is given, for example: 'At present we answer 83% of 999 calls within 15 seconds.' It is here that various overlaps in the quality assurance approach begin to emerge, because standards for answering telephone calls appear in the charters of many police forces which have not gone through the full *Meeting Community Expectations* process. Furthermore, how far the local standard for answering 999 calls has been met is one of the Audit Commission's PIs. The results from the monitoring of performance in meeting these standards are becoming available on a monthly basis in Leicestershire and the results and the standards are reviewed quarterly.

About 20 standards for the management of crime key service area have been developed. Organized under the acronym CRIME (care and reassurance; recording and representing information; investigating, maintaining contact; enabling victims) they will cover areas shown by the surveys to be important to the public and of concern to police officers themselves. Amongst the standards set, therefore, will be procedures for the collection and processing of information and deadlines for supplying 'Victims of crime' leaflets, referrals to crime support units, and information on the progress of the investigation. A series of 'one-liners', rather than the full standards, will probably be published under the *Policing Charter* and, instead of producing baselines, the results from the first assessments of performance in meeting the standards will become the benchmarks. Monitoring performance will be a major problem for several reasons. These include the large number of standards, which means that whilst some of the standards will be covered by existing PIs, and other could be either monitored by changing what is asked for in crime reports or covered by surveys of the victims of crime, for yet others annual spot checks may have to be used. It will also mean extending monitoring into areas previously left very much to the discretion of the individual officer.

The significant feature of developments in Leicestershire is that there has been an overall approach to quality so that performance management and the corporate strategy are being driven by the *Policing Charter* and the purposes and aims set out in it. The whole process, including the standards, is approved by the Quality of Service Working Group of the Police Committee. The intention is to use the standards as part of the continuous process, through monitoring and review, to develop services that meet community expectations. The performance management system will ensure that the PIs required by HMIC, ACPO and the Audit Commission will be incorporated into the overall system of force PIs and the monitoring of performance in meeting the standard. Performance management and the development of a corporate strategy will also mean that areas where standards are not being adequately met (and where PIs appear to reveal poor performance in aspects of quality such as value for money and effective use of resources) will be targets for action in a process involving sub-divisions in the formulation of targets. Public satisfaction levels with specific services will be monitored regularly and the longitudinal pattern will influence the area that require targeting. Whilst rising public expectations might create problems the system is geared up to react to this as far as possible, and the marketing of the results achieved within the resources constraints will be one method used in the attempt to dampen down unrealistic expectations.

Note

I would like to thank all those in Leicestershire Constabulary without whose generous help this case study could not have been written. Responsibility for any errors lies with the author.

PART THREE

OVERVIEW

11

Improvement Strategies

Christopher Pollitt

The ingredients of improvement

In this chapter we seek to accomplish two tasks. First, we aim to review the eight case studies in order to relate them more closely to the logical model of a quality improvement process which we built up in Chapters 1 and 2. Secondly, we intend to frame this reconsideration of the details of quality processes by setting it within a broader analysis of organizational strategies, cultures and circumstances.

It is clear from the arguments developed in Chapters 1 and 2 that any fully fledged attempt to improve the quality of public services must confront a number of challenging requirements. Logically, these requirements can be summarized as the ingredients, or steps, in a model process, and we set them out in this way in Table 11.1.

There are a number of points we need to discuss concerning this model, but perhaps the most important of all is to note that it is not yet a *strategy*. Our model is, as indicated above, like a list of

Table 11.1 *A ten-step model for quality improvement*

1   Decide and make explicit the purposes of the effort to improve quality.
2   Conceptualize and define quality.
3   Operationalize the concept so as to be able to construct measures and indicators.
4   Collect the data necessary to assign values to the indicators.
5   Process the data.
6   Interpret and evaluate the indicator data.
7   Determine the consequences of the evaluation in terms of organizational learning, organizational legitimacy and possible policy change.
8   Select actions to adjust organizational performance (for example, additional training, improved provision of information, altering incentive structures for staff, devising new mechanisms for user participation)
9   Give public account of steps 6, 7 and 8.
10 Go back to step 4, 3, 2, or 1 (whichever is most appropriate) and restart the cycle.

Table 11.2   *Elements in an organizational strategy*

(a)	*A statement of guiding values*, say the satisfaction of users' needs (for an advice bureau) or the provision of a stable and caring environment (for services to the elderly mentally ill). This is sometimes referred to as a 'mission statement'.
(b)	*Rules for strategic resource allocation* which reinforce the statement of guiding values.
(c)	*Prescriptions for the key operating structures and processes of the organization.* The structures might include the divisional or unit structure and the processes would include, *inter alia*, recruitment and disciplinary procedures as well as those key processes in which the organization interacted with its users/customers.
(d)	*Regulatory and monitoring systems* to ensure that the guiding values are indeed being pursued, processes are being followed and resources are actually being targeted in such a way as to realize the 'mission'. These are mechanisms for 'keeping on course'.
(e)	*Specification of a set of processes by which individual and organizational learning and change are expected to take place.* This is perhaps the most dynamic aspect of a strategy, and is aimed at producing 'course change' rather than simply 'keeping on course'. It concerns a special set of organizational processes, conceptually distinct (though in practice overlapping) with the standard operating processes identified in (c) and the regulatory systems identified at (d). These *learning processes* will particularly concern the main sources of available feedback on how the organization is doing. They should be adequate to facilitate changes in resource allocation, organizational structures and processes and regulatory/monitoring systems.

ingredients, set out in logical order. A strategy, however, is more like a recipe: it should also include hints on how to handle the ingredients, how to present the meal, common pitfalls to watch out for during the cooking process and so on. In other words the process model delineates a set of logical requirements and relationships while the strategy enfolds these within a broader plan to deal with the manifold uncertainties and complexities – local and global – of the real world. It relates a discrete effort at quality improvement to everything else that may be going on in the kitchen, that is to the overall running of the organization.

Thus our conceptualization of *strategy* is one which is action oriented and encompassing of the whole organization. A complete strategy consists of at least five principal elements, as depicted in Table 11.2.

Thus a strategy enfolds and 'brings to life' the ten logical steps set out in this chapter. It is important to understand the relationship between the ten-step model and the strategy. The model, in effect, comprises a set of learning and monitoring processes. It may therefore be regarded as part of element (e) of an organization's strategy, that is learning and changing course, although once a quality process is up and running it also contributes significantly to elements (c) and (d). In other words, in so far as steps 1 to 8 of the model lead to policy and process change, quality improvement has most to do with learning element of strategy. This is an important insight into the nature of quality improvement and contradicts the frequent perception by some staff at the beginning of quality improvement efforts that what is involved is just 'tightening up' and getting everyone to follow more precisely a set of predetermined procedures.

Each type of strategy will tend to generate a different emphasis as between the different steps in the model, because the guiding values and purposes are different (strategy element (a)). We will see this as we (next) examine each of the ten steps with an eye to both strategic and more detailed operational concerns.

Finally, the chapter will conclude with a more general overview of the problem of choosing a strategy in such a way as realistically to *match purposes to circumstances*. Note the importance of the word 'circumstances' here. The most appropriate strategy for an organization to adopt will vary not only with its purposes but also with where it starts from, that is its circumstances. For example, a strategy that is optimal for a predominantly clerical operation that has until now done little to systematize quality assurance is unlikely to suit another organization which employs professional groups that have already articulated elaborate systems of peer review.

In short, the ten-step model only comes fully alive when set within an organizational strategy. But there is no 'one best strategy': the most appropriate strategy choice will be influenced by the organization's mission, the characteristics of the service it provides, and the circumstances at the time and location at which the strategy is formulated (Figure 11.1)

Step 1: the purposes of quality improvement efforts

The very first step in the model is that of making explicit the purpose of quality measurement. As Chapters 1 and 2 indicated, the precise purpose may vary. It is always important to ask which group or groups are intended to be the prime or immediate beneficiaries of the attempt to improve quality.

One category of quality improvement effort is essentially concerned with improving the producer's control over the characteristics of the product or service. Many early quality improvement efforts in manufacturing industry were of this type. Managements in manufacturing organizations knew what they wanted (or though they did) so

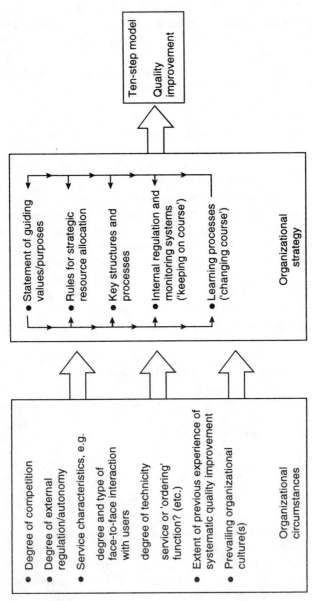

Figure 11.1   *Circumstances, strategy and quality improvement*

they installed inspection or monitoring systems to achieve tighter control over what was actually happening on the production lines. The final users or consumers of the product or service may eventually have benefited from these efforts but they were in no sense directly a part of them. More than anything else they represented an attempt by senior management to tighten their grip on what production operatives were doing. The focus was on what we have termed *producer quality*. In the public sector this kind of approach has frequently been associated with the general pressure to control costs and increase the productivity of public services.

Different in spirit, approach and tactics are attempts directly to improve *user satisfaction*. Whereas strategies to improve producer quality tend to be founded on the assumption that the producer already knows what 'quality' is, this same assumption has to be abandoned if the main focus is going to be on user satisfaction. Here, the only way to know what constitutes quality is to ask the users themselves. Only they can tell the producer/provider which are the characteristics of the service which they value the most, and which should therefore be the target for efforts at measurement and standard setting.

There is a third, hybrid purpose – one that has perhaps become especially common in the public services sector. It is to enhance the *legitimacy* of the providing authority. We refer to this as a hybrid because although it is ostensibly focused on user (or, more broadly, citizens') perceptions, it is at root concerned with the self-interest of the producer. Thus politicians who wish to stay in office may push for superficial and short-term measures (glossy leaflets, redecorated waiting rooms, new staff uniforms) in an effort to convince the public that a service is being improved. This is *not* to suggest that the quest for democratic legitimacy is necessarily just a public relations exercise. More fundamental and long-term quality improvement efforts may also be undertaken by governments anxious to retain the trust of their citizens and the popularity of basic public services.

Several contemporary approaches to quality improvement (including TQM) embody a strong preference for the second of the above purposes, that is user satisfaction. We share this preference, but would also concede that in many public service contexts user satisfaction cannot be the *only* consideration in the setting of quality standards (Steward, 1992; Clapham, 1993). Indeed, in some cases this criterion cannot easily be applied at all. For example, the taxpayer frequently has to be considered alongside the user, perhaps especially in those cases where a public service is provided free to users, or at least at a price well below cost. Tax-funded health care services are one example of this type. Elsewhere the problem deepens: a service may be supplied actually *against the wishes* of immediate users, as in the case of a motorist whose vehicle fails a compulsory roadworthiness check or a resident who applies for but is denied planning permission to make an alteration to her property. Stewart (1992) has described these public sector functions as 'social ordering' rather than 'service providing'. The prime beneficiaries of such services may be individuals who never 'use' them, or may be the community at large or possibly future generations (where an environmental project begins to restore a polluted area).

Even where the individual users of a service are readily identifiable they may sometimes be unable to express rational or coherent assessments of service quality. Examples here would include services to the elderly mentally ill, or services with a very high technical content (brain surgery, advanced fire-fighting) where the general user can see the outcome but may be poorly equipped to judge whether the technical quality of service was good (the patient may die despite technically brilliant surgery; the fire may be put out despite technical errors and incompetence by the fire service).

In sum, not all quality improvement efforts have the same mixture of purposes and not all service contexts permit the identification of a well-defined group of users whose preferences can then be tapped to provide unambiguous help with steps 2, 3 and 4 of the quality improvement model in Table 11.1. Even where user assessments are obtainable they may not be the only consideration that needs to be taken into account when quality standards are being set.

Our case studies also illustrate how easy it can be to overlook the first step altogether – or at least leave it in only a vague and general form. Quality improvement appears to be such a virtuous activity that it may seem pedantic to question exactly why or for whom it is being undertaken. Thus, for example, the purposes of the improvements in Duisburg (Chapter 5) remain rather diffuse. Helmut Klages notes that German local government reforms have in general been concerned with establishing co-operative relations with citizens, science and the economy and social institutions, but this is extremely broad. The specific purposes of the reforms in Duisburg are bound up with the concept of an 'enterprise city', but this, too, is a fairly abstract concept, open to a variety of interpretations. Or again, the creation of more locally responsible services in Harlow (Chapter 6) may originally have been undertaken as much to try to preserve the local authority's direct services organization (DSO) as to satisfy user wishes. 'Quality' appears to have been a somewhat subordinate (though perfectly genuine) concern within a broader programme of decentralization and democratization, itself partly triggered by the external threat of losing the DSO.

More commonly, perhaps, purposes *are* quite clearly stated, but they are multiple. For example, the French DDE reforms (Chapter 4) were undertaken both to motivate staff and in response to client demands. The pilot project on quality at four Swedish institutions of higher education was launched to assist quality improvement efforts at the individual institutions *and* to permit inter-institutional comparisons (Chapter 7).The innovations at the Dutch National Logistic Command were made as an adjustment to financial cuts, but also to improve the quality of the logistical and maintenance service (Chapter 9). In all these cases a crucial question is, 'how are the different purposes to be weighted and combined, one against another?' Our argument here is not that multiple purposes are somehow wrong (that would be hopelessly unrealistic) but that communicating them successfully requires great clarity (and honesty) on the part of politicians and managers alike. Public services staff – whose co-operation will be essential to the success of most improvement efforts – quickly detect the tensions between (say) cost-cutting and raising user satisfaction, and are less likely to lend their full support to an initiative that claims to be all about the latter but is actually also very much aiming at the former.

The cases studies show how quality initiatives seldom enjoy the luxury of standing alone as the exclusive focus of interest and effort. In Harlow quality was allied with decentralization efforts (Chapter 6). In Duisburg quality improvement was part of a wider response to economic decline (Chapter 5). For Leicestershire Constabulary quality became bound up with a more general national concern over falling public confidence in the police and with the government's *Policing Charter* (Chapter 10). In the Netherlands the quality improvements analysed by Mol were set within a larger context of the 'peace dividend' and the consequent reduction in the scale of the armed forces (Chapter 9).

Thus, in the politicized context of public service provision, quality improvement efforts very frequently need to accommodate themselves to other, competing agendas. Those charged with the design and implementation of quality improvement programmes would be well advised to scan the political environment and seek to identify other initiatives with which co-operation of this kind may be possible. In the real world of the public sector, unlike the TQM textbooks, programmes of quality improvement will rarely be dominant and all-encompassing. More commonly they will have to share the stage with a variety of other reform initiatives. In such situations the careful choosing of allies may create synergies and add political 'weight' to the quality improvers' cause.

Step 2: conceptualize the model

Some of our examples show an admirable degree of attention being given to this stage of conceptualization. Leicestershire Constabulary, for example, self-consciously focused on community (user) expectations and identified five key service areas in which delivery standards were to be defined. The Dutch Ministry of Defence adopted the QMbO definition of 'the whole of the attributes and characteristics of a product or service relevant to the fulfilment of stated or evident needs'. In Chapter 3 van Vught and Westerheijden indicate that their own approach is in terms of 'fitness for purposes', though they recognize that purposes themselves will vary between the main stakeholder groups.

Other cases, however, such as Harlow Council and the Swedish school project, seem to have fought shy of adherence to any single, stipulative definition. A sympathetic commentator might say that their approach to conceptualization was formative, participative and exploratory whereas an unsympathetic critic could argue that the lack of a single, explicitly stated concept handicapped the improvement efforts and led to somewhat unfocused activities that were not always tied to clear standards.

Overall it might be said that one crucial watershed is between, on the one hand, those strategies which encourage active user participation in the *definition* of quality (and its salient dimensions, such as in Leicestershire Constabulary, Chapter 10) and, on the other, those which fix the definition internally (on the producer/provider side, such as in the NHS study reported by Joss in Chapter 8). In the latter cases providers *may* subsequently choose to seek user values for degrees of satisfaction with (internally predetermined) quality dimensions, but those dimensions will not themselves have been chosen by users. In certain circumstances this may be the only way, for example if there are no identifiable individual 'users' of a service or where the 'understandability' of a service to its users is low. In many other circumstances, however, there is a choice as to how early and how far to involve users.

Where users are involved at step 2 there are both benefits and costs. The benefits are that providers can enjoy increased confidence that the dimensions of quality chosen for operationalization *are* in fact those which are most salient for the users of the service. The obvious costs are the time and resources expended on eliciting user conceptualizations ('appraisal' costs in terms of Chapter 8). Such costs will vary somewhat with the methods used. Current research suggests that there is no 'one best method' for all circumstances (Brunel University, 1993). Focus groups can be very useful in providing a first broad identification of relevant dimensions, but more detailed work will be required if trade-offs between different dimensions of quality are to be established (such as between speed of service and accuracy of service). Stated preference approaches are often the least-worst approach to establishing such trade-offs, but even these have their limitations (Brunel University, 1993). PC software is now available to enable researchers to conduct and analyse stated preference surveys quite quickly.

There can be another, less obvious kind of cost. The service provider can experience – or at least fear – a certain loss of power, of control. After all, users are now allowed 'in on the act' where previously the provider organization could make up its own mind. Managers and professionals can easily become uneasy about this, despite the existence of offsetting benefits.

All this assumes that users are both readily identifiable and reasonably homogeneous in their views. If different groups of users have radically different 'conceptual maps' of a service (and different trade-offs between attributes) then there will be a need for expressly political judgements to be made about the relative weightings to be given to different and diverging interests. Such radical differences may be most common in respect to 'social ordering' tasks such as inspecting, licensing and maintaining public order, where one group of citizens are being restrained from their desired behaviours in order to protect other groups.

Steps 3 and 4: operationalize into measures and indicators and collect data

These two steps are, for the sake of brevity, here collapsed into one. Clearly, the precise way in which the conceptualization of the chosen quality concept is undertaken will determine what types of data need to be collected.

Not surprisingly, our set of case studies yields a considerable diversity of methods. One rule of thumb might be that the greater the role accorded to users in the definition of quality (see preceding section), the more complex and varied may need to be the modes of operationalization and data collection. Thus, for example, the prominent role accorded to users in the police study (Chapter 10) meant that Leicestershire Constabulary was obliged to embark upon participatory exercises to establish standards, regular surveys of public satisfaction with particular services (building up a longitudinal series) and extensive internal monitoring of services as delivered (to check how far standards were being achieved). By contrast the NHS study (Chapter 8) did not involve end users at all, and was able to confine itself to a fairly rough-and-ready costing of a limited number of types of non-conformance to expectations. Even here, however, the improvers needed to survey the perceptions held by staff in 13 other departments within the hospital, and to organize brainstorming sessions with the staff on the ward at the focus of the pilot in order to identify a shortlist of key issues. The lesson seems to be that even internally focused efforts at increasing control of the production process may require considerable fresh data to be collected.

The remaining case studies are distributed right across the spectrum from high user participation to virtually none at all. The Swedish higher education study (Chapter 7) did collect some data direct from students (one category of end user) but this was only one of several sources for the self-evaluation which formed the first stage of the pilot. The second stage was an expert report – essentially a form of external peer review in which end users played no direct part. In France-Télécom performance indicators were developed centrally, without much attention to the wishes of individual clients. In the DDE case, however, surveys of client opinion played an important part, though these 'clients' were themselves politicians rather than citizen end users (Chapter 4). In the Harlow case (Chapter 6) local residents were involved in contract specification and monitoring (which are, in effect, forms of quality operationalization and data collection) and a neighbourhood forum was set up to encourage participation. This sounds as though it had the potential to develop into a user-driven approach to quality, though evidently that had not always been the priority.

Towards the lower end of the participation spectrum come the German and Dutch studies (Chapters 5 and 9). In the German case regular consultation with another stakeholder – *employees* rather than citizens – appears to have been the prominent feature. For the Dutch logistics organization task programmes were determined more by the wishes of military superiors than by the organization's immediate customers, internal or external. In the study of Harlow

Council (Chapter 6) Gaster argues that it is important to make use of the grass-roots knowledge of front-line service delivery staff, that this is often valuable data in itself and that taking it seriously also helps legitimate those staff. Whilst we would agree that this kind of information can be very valuable (the grass-roots staff often know about problems long before top management, and develop a more subtle understanding of their nature) we must also acknowledge that making use of it is often less than straightforward. If grass-roots staff knowledge is to be integrated with other streams of data then the overall improvement strategy will need to make two kinds of provision. First, at step 3 front-line staff will have to be consulted and their own conceptualizations of quality taken into account. Secondly, thought will need to be given to how information that is frequently qualitative, impressionistic and informal can be systematically gathered without intruding too bureaucratically into the activities of these same staff. Recent technological developments such as portable electronic notepads (the contents of which can later be uploaded into organization-wide IT systems) may offer possibilities here.

The extent of stakeholder participation is certainly one important issue in operationalization and data collection, but it is far from the only one. Another is the very extent of measurement itself. In the early stages of quality improvement there can appear to be a tension between *measuring* and staff *motivation* (winning hearts and minds over to the drive for better quality). Very commonly staff are anxious about or even directly resistant to the measurement of their activities. There is therefore a temptation for management to soft-pedal on measurement at first whilst putting the main effort into cultural change efforts (hearts and minds). We regard this as a dangerous strategy. Winning hearts and minds is certainly a crucial part of the process of creating a new approach to service quality. However, to imply to staff that this is likely to be accomplished without quite intimate and challenging measurement and review is either naïve or less than honest. Quality improvement without measurement is a land in which wishful thinking is a constant temptation. We have encountered a number of experienced senior managers in public service organizations who, looking back on several years of quality improvement efforts, have expressed the wish that their organizations had placed more emphasis on measurement at the very beginning. Edwardsson et al. (1994: 245) put it as follows: 'Managers and staff need external standards and reference points, as well as their own goals and standards', and go on to recommend functional benchmarking.

Following from this are some equally sensitive issues of *comparison*. Many public services are delivered by a set of broadly similar local units – schools, for example, hospitals, fire brigades, social security offices or police forces. In such situations considerations of public accountability are likely to generate a demand for measurements that will facilitate inter-unit comparisons: how the response times for this fire brigade compare with those of other brigades in the region or country, and so on (see step 9 below). The need for such comparisons (often termed benchmarking) carries with it strong implications for data collection. Basically it creates a need for some kind of nationally uniform data set, and thereby sets limits (though not necessarily terribly onerous ones) to local variety and creativity.

Van Vught and Westerheijden (Chapter 3) address precisely this issue. Approaching higher education at the level of a system rather than of individual institutions, they argue for the creation of a *managing agent* to look after the quality dimensions of the entire system. A prime task of such a body would be the promulgation of a minimum set of procedures, formats and data sets which all institutions would be obliged to use in measuring and reporting quality. This minimum set would *not* prevent individual institutions within the system from collecting additional data or using other formats or procedures *as local additions*. It would, however, give the government and the public a minimum data set by which comparisons of individual institutions within the system could be made. It is interesting to speculate whether this type of institutional device could be applied in other sectors – health care, for example, or social services. In the UK, for example, at national level the Audit Commission has been given the role of developing, in consultation with local authorities, a set of common performance indicators which, when published, will demonstrate how far each local authority is achieving standards for quality and other aspects of performance set within the *Citizen's Charter* programme (Audit Commission, 1992). In France, Trosa argues (Chapter 4) for *both* 'general, simple and compulsory indicators' *and* local 'indicators to control quality developed by the services themselves'. It would seem that there is some common ground here.

Finally, we may address the issue of the relationship between quality and cost. Whilst, on the one hand, it is important to separate quality improvement from cost-saving exercises (and to maintain a healthy distance between the concepts of quality and efficiency), on the other hand management will nevertheless need to develop a reasonably precise idea of the costs as well as the benefits of quality improvement activities. Joss (Chapter 8) makes a very useful distinction between appraisal costs, prevention costs, internal failure costs and external failure costs. Only if data on all four types of cost are collected can management see the overall balance between savings (on the 'costs of non-conformity') and expenditures (on quality control appraisals and quality assurance procedures). As Joss indicates, however, measures of the costs of non-conformity are actually (as yet) quite rare. Even his own study concentrates on only one of the four types of cost (internal failures). Or again, in the Dutch NLC study (Chapter 9), Mol points out that the NLC's cost accounting system does not permit costing of the 'effects' achieved by the new system. Without this kind of cost data, quality improvement efforts are more likely to remain on the margins of organizational strategies – nice things to be doing but seemingly not absolutely essential to the basic business of balancing the budget and achieving efficiency or 'cost improvement' targets.

Steps 5 and 6: process and interpret the data

Processing the data may seem quite a straightforward matter, devoid of much analytical content. To some extent this is true, but even the relatively mechanical business of data processing can hold some significant implications for the management of quality improvement. Interpretation, by contrast, is hardly ever straightforward, and deserves very close attention indeed.

One problem which is quickly encountered is the vastness of the potential processing operation. Even if one concentrates on a purely technical, management-driven concept of quality the possible number of technical aspects may be very large. This can clearly be seen where services have been put out to contract. For example, contractual specifications for cutting grass in public parks and on roadsides can become fearsomely complex and long-winded, attempting to define exactly how long the grass should be, how often it should be cut in different categories of public space, what should be done about weeds or litter, and so on.

As one moves towards user-driven definitions, the specification of quality may become even more elaborate, partly because a service provider may be trying to accommodate the varying wishes of a range of different stakeholders (see steps 3 and 4 above). Thus the sheer volume of data to be processed rapidly escalates and the need for specialist data processing staff to integrate the different flows of data becomes more salient.

Handling a high volume of data becomes a more acute problem still during step 6 – interpretation. Typically citizens will require not just the bare quantitative data but a good deal of background explanation as well (Robertson Bell Associates, 1993). The resulting document (many indicators, many comparisons, much explanatory text) soon becomes bulky. Bulky documents are themselves expensive to produce and distribute, and may be somewhat off-putting to many readers. There is an obvious trade-off here between comprehensiveness (more information) and impact (a few, key measures presented in an easily digestible way). An oscillation over time between misleading simplicity and unintelligible complexity has been a feature of performance indicator systems as far apart as Soviet central economic planning and the UK National Health Service (Pollitt, 1990; see also Carter et al., 1992).

The process of interpretation is inherently problematic because, as Trosa indicates (Chapter 4), 'each indicator has a potential for bias'. The best antidote to bias is probably a combination of some sort of independent meta-level agency of the kind proposed by van Vught and Westerheijden (to set common formats and data collection procedures) with open publication (to ensure public debate involving a range of stakeholders, each with their own interpretative perspective). If data have been gathered from a variety of stakeholders (as will almost inevitably be the case with more participative approaches to the operationalization of quality) then the authority publishing the data can check its own interpretations against those of the other stakeholders while the document is still in draft and withheld from the public domain. This practice is already common in higher education, as Chapter 3 made clear. Of course, this may result in the finally published document containing a variety of stated interpretations, side by side, but such practices are gradually becoming more acceptable. In the United States, for example, official mortality tables for Medicare hospitals were, from the mid 1980s, published including interpretative comments from the hospitals themselves set alongside the figures gathered by the federal authorities. In the UK in 1994 the publication by central government of the first set of national quality indicators for National Health Service hospitals resulted in a barrage of statements by individual hospitals claiming to show why apparently low scores should not be regarded as truly indicative of poor quality. Unsurprisingly, those hospitals which scored well on the new system appeared much less energetic in offering alternative interpretations!

Finally, not all interpretative problems arise from bias or vested interest. Even in a bias-free world it can be extremely difficult to decide whether a given value for measured performance was principally the result of the decisions and choices of the organization under examination, or, by contrast, the unavoidable consequence of organizational circumstance (the circumstances/strategy distinction of Figure 11.1). The case of the Dutch NLC showed that it was hard to interpret the TAPRO indicator data because the circumstances in which they were generated had been one of constant reorganization and general workload reduction across Dutch land forces as a whole. Was it these more general circumstances that had influenced indicator values, or the more specific actions of the maintenance units?

Steps 7 and 8: determining consequences and selecting actions

After meanings (interpretation) come consequences and, after consequences, actions. It might be thought that by this stage, with so many earlier decisions taken (concerning concepts, methods, data and so on), the remaining steps would be straightforward – simply a matter of following through what had gone before. Nothing could be further from the truth. Steps 7 and 8 of the model still contain many choices.

In fact the steps of determining consequences and taking actions are precisely those where the *rest* of an organization's activities come back into focus – where what may hitherto have been 'just' a quality initiative is obliged to accommodate itself to other elements within the prevailing strategy. Thus, for example, the impact of their fairly elaborate quality mechanisms created within the Dutch NLC were limited by larger features of the organization such as lack of accompanying decentralization and the continuing prevalence of a strong military hierarchy (Chapter 9). This observation leads us to the more general point that quality improvement efforts frequently prompt considerations of organizational restructuring (Edwardsson et al., 1994: 245).Such restructuring can be low level and local or high level and transformational for the entire organization. This latter type of restructuring takes us back to the strategic level, and we will have more to say about it in the final sections of this chapter.

In the Swedish higher education study it was determined that the university departments concerned needed to focus more sharply on particular areas of excellence, and on pedagogics, but according to Westlund (Chapter 7) little of the necessary action was actually taken, partly because of inadequate marketing of the study and partly because of cultural resistance to its messages. Another way of expressing this would be to say that in the end the Swedish quality pilot simply wasn't given much importance within the universities' overall strategies – although a few years later this may have been beginning to change. In managerial terms no one seems to have been given specific responsibility for developing a plan for implementing the findings of the study. Perhaps this is a typical weakness where universities are concerned: they are used to conducting research and engaging in debate, but less comfortable with settling down to choose one particular course of action and assigning executive responsibility to a named individual for carrying it out.

The Swedish example therefore raises the more general issue of *implementation*. Current management doctrines urge that, in the early stages at least, responsibility for quality improvements should be firmly and visibly lodged with one or more named individuals in each unit. Such a solution has an appealing simplicity to it, but also immediately raises a number of further questions. The first of these is whether the named 'quality person' should have a primarily facilitative role, or an executive one. In British universities, for example, facilitative roles are common. The same is true for the National Health Service. These are both organizations where strong professional groupings have struggled to preserve a collegial approach to the conduct of business, continuing to allow wide discretion to the individual doctor or academic. By contrast (still in the UK) Post Office Counters Ltd, when implementing a TQM-style initiative, took a conscious decision to create senior quality support managers who were executive managers, not just facilitators. The second issue is the extent to which quality improvement roles can and should be combined with other management tasks, particularly day-to-day operational management. Again, opinions differ. Post Office Counters Ltd has recently reorganized into a structure divided into key business processes, and within each process quality improvement is the responsibility of an individual who is *not* also burdened with responsibility for day-to-day management. This kind of separation has the very significant advantage that it protects quality improvement issues from being constantly pushed aside by the pressure of routine business. The danger, however, is that rank and file staff (and other managers) will come to regard quality improvement as something which is someone else's responsibility, not theirs. Thus a key task for any specially appointed quality manager (or facilitator) will be to spread the understanding that, in a profound sense, *everyone* in the organization is responsible for quality.

One of the most common consequences of quality initiatives is the discovery or refinement of training needs. This was very clearly stated in the Duisburg study and in the case of the Leicestershire police (Chapters 5 and 10). Management needs to decide how this is to be approached. Should the training process be 'top-down' or 'bottom-up'? Should it be mainly provided by expert quality tutors and consultants brought in from outside, or by the organization's own staff, or by some mixture of the two? There are obvious dangers to be avoided here. Buying in a few higher paid consultants to give a few seminars and training sessions will, *by itself*, do very little to implant quality consciousness into an organization. There are too many other organizational demands, incentives and penalties competing for the attention of staff. If training *is* provided by outside experts (and this may in fact be very sensible, especially in the early stages, when an organization may not yet have much in-house expertise) then it needs to be quickly supported by back-up and actions which develop 'ownership' within the organization. Supporting quality improvement in this way may certainly have the wider implications referred to at the beginning of this section. New quality roles may need to be created, pay and promotion arrangements may require adjustment to reflect achievements in improving quality, the rapid feedback to all staff of data concerning the standards of service achieved should be a high priority – and so on (Edwardsson et al., 1994: 245). Training cannot stand alone, and cannot simply be left to bought-in experts. Some public service organizations have used 'cascade' systems, where a senior level of managers are trained in new quality improvement procedures and are also trained themselves to train the next level of staff beneath them. Such a system has considerable advantages but, again, there are possible drawbacks which should be watched for. Cascades tend to be only as strong as their weakest link. There will probably be some 'unbelievers' in the system – managers who are cynical or resistant to the new procedures for quality improvement. If these individuals are expected to train others they are very likely to communicate their negative attitudes (and if they are themselves at a fairly senior level they have the potential to 'blight' a substantial part of the organization). Thus, if a cascade system is to be adopted and the organization is really serious about making it a success, then it will also need to set up mechanisms for retraining and counselling the (hopefully few) unbelievers. If these individuals remain resistant to the new procedures then ultimately the organization may need to move them to other posts, or even require them to leave the organization. Such moves, though needing very careful and sensitive handling, can send powerful signals through the rest of the organization that indicate the seriousness with which senior management regard the quality strategy as a whole.

Resources, as always, are crucial. Unfortunately there is sometimes a tendency for public service organizations to underestimate
and underinvest in quality training. In a major study of TQM pilot
schemes in the British National Health Service a research team
compared the approach at NHS sites with that adopted at two
commercial organizations. They came to the conclusion that:

> in many respects, the NHS appeared to be less successful at this stage of its
> implementations than the commercial companies ... It is also clear that
> funding of TQM at the NHS sites, while not inconsiderable, was a whole
> order of magnitude lower than the two commercial companies concerned
> ... These benefits were also underpinned by a general seriousness of
> purpose and understanding of TQM that appeared to span a much
> broader base of staff than we found at most NHS TQM sites. (CEPPP,
> 1994: 37)

In so far as quality improvement requires either attitudinal change or
the learning of new skills (or both) training is likely to constitute one
of the key actions, especially in the early stages. Since most
significant quality improvement efforts will embody *precisely* these
two requirements it is necessary for management to understand at the
outset that substantial training expenditure is almost inevitable.

The issue of allocating resources to training for quality improvement is actually but a small part of a much broader and more complex
allocation problem, and one which has some uniquely public sector
aspects to it. Let us suppose that quality data have been collected for
a whole national system of public service provider units (schools,
social security offices, hospitals and so on). Let us further suppose
that these data show that some units are delivering high-quality
services, others middling-quality and some very low-quality. Assuming that the available resources are severely limited (a safe assumption in most parts of most public sectors these days) *where* should the
funds earmarked for quality improvement be applied?

One possibility is clearly that resources should be put into the
poorest-performing units so as to raise minimum standards. On the
other hand this could be seen as rewarding failure, and there is a case
for giving funding priority to the best-performing units, so as to
reward success and motivate others to copy the best practice. The
business yardstick of profit maximization is not available for solving
this dilemma: indeed, in respect of public services the problem gets
more complex still, because the public themselves are likely to be
interested in a whole series of other criteria, such as equity and
fairness. One common argument would be that any money available
for quality improvement should be equally distributed across all units

(though this gives no incentive to the best performers to continue their special efforts and no incentive to the poor performers to embark on fundamental change). Another popular view might be that resources should be distributed according to the measured need of local populations for the services in question – so that, for example, communities with the greatest proneness to ill-health received the largest per capita share of health service funding. A third possibility might be that priority in funding should be given to units where the services delivered had demonstrably the greatest *effect* (this is different from both a criterion of need and a criterion of high-quality service).

In short, there are a number of rival principles upon which allocation decisions could be founded. Choice of a particular criterion, or combination of them, is one of the most quintessentially *political* decisions there is. Yet the private sector quality handbooks scarcely even address it. Here, therefore, is a major strategic issue.

Steps 9 and 10: giving a public account and returning to the beginning of the loop

Public accountability is another feature of public services which distinguishes them from private sector, for-profit firms. Some commentators occasionally liken the accountability of public leaders to parliaments and the citizenry to the accountability of the directors of a firm to its shareholders, but this analogy is false and inadequate (Pollitt, 1993: Chapter 5). Public accountability may be subdivided into political accountability and managerial accountability (Day and Klein, 1987) and quality improvement involves both.

Political accountability is an accountability for broad policies and for the values which inform those policies. It also includes accountability for the justice, fairness and timeliness of specific decisions and for general standards of probity in public life. Political accountability is difficult to discharge, not least because it is accountability to a spectrum of groups (the 'public') which are themselves likely to possess divergent interests and values. Because of the party-competitive nature of liberal democracies it is also accountability conducted against the background of constant rivalry, criticism and pressure from opposition groups who are themselves seeking to take power or at least discomfort those who currently hold power.

Managerial accountability is more narrowly defined, being accountability for the discharge of defined tasks. The manager of a local social security office cannot be blamed if current social security policy is harsh and inequitable (that is a matter for the political accountability of the government) but he or she can be held responsible for mistakes made in the processing of claims, for long queues, unpleasant conditions in the waiting room, aggressive attitudes on the part of counter staff, and so on.

Major quality improvement efforts in the public services sector usually involve both elements of public accountability. Many of our case studies do not, however, give much attention to the matter of rendering a public account. In some instances this is because the project described is only a pilot, at an early stage. In others the focus is mainly internal and managerial. Nevertheless, a few cases do mention aspects of public accountability. In the Leicestershire police study Hanney points out that the public presentation of 'results' needs to be carefully handled so as to avoid any unrealistic inflation of public expectations concerning the services in question. Presentation was also an issue in Westlund's study of Swedish universities, where weaknesses in this process are said to have contributed to the unresponsiveness of institutional leaders to the findings. In local government research reported elsewhere it was discovered that residents in a particular English borough wanted quality information validated by an independent body and published in a distinctive, single document with good background explanations for the statistics and plenty of comparisons with other local authorities (Robertson Bell Associates, 1993). In this case public expectations were actually quite low, at least in the sense that they did not trust the local authority itself to present figures in an unbiased way.

A major question is raised by van Vught and Westerheijden in their analysis of higher education systems. They ask whether *all* quality data should be published, or only some. They point out that staff may be less open in their self-evaluations if they know that anything they say or discuss will be released to the public domain. On the other hand, politicians and the public may well be suspicious of a system in which only selected and summary figures are published, and the detail is kept confidential. The balance that is to be struck in such issues (which affect many if not most public services, not just universities) is one that needs to be decided at an early stage, so that the participants know the 'rules of the game' and are not surprised or disappointed by later decisions.

In short, the rendering of a public account is a complex matter, usually involving several different audiences and two or more different levels. It is inherently unlikely that one form of dissemination will suit each potential audience, for example members of a parliament or national assembly, the general public, users of the service concerned, or staff in the service delivery organization. Users, for example, may want detailed practical information about how far local service standards are being met and previous problems with, say, access to a service are being tackled. Taxpayer citizens may be more interested in reassuring themselves that a service is giving reasonable value for money – that there is evidence that its goals are being achieved and without unwarranted escalation in its costs. Politicians will also be interested in value for money, but may also wish to debate the fundamental goals of a service and to test whether a service is meeting criteria such as geographical equity, equal opportunities and fairness of procedures.

The final step – returning to step 1, 2, 3 or 4 of the model – is fairly self-explanatory. If, when the data have been processed and interpreted, and public account has been given, service quality is seen to be broadly satisfactory, then those responsible may simply return to step 4 and commence the next annual cycle. If, however, it can be seen that certain significant aspects of quality are not being captured by the existing range of measures, then it will be more appropriate to return to step 3 (in order to invent new measures) or even step 2 (if a more fundamental reappraisal of the concept seems to be needed). Finally, it may be that the results of going through the cycle are such that a deep reconsideration of the very purposes of the quality improvement programme becomes necessary. In this case the organization returns to step 1 and begins to rethink its entire strategy.

Overview: choosing a strategy for quality improvement

At the beginning of this chapter we suggested that organizational circumstances constrained the types of strategy that any given organization could realistically pursue, and that the chosen strategy would itself then influence how quality improvement could be approached (Figure 11.1). To put it another way, the very first step in our ten-step logical model is usually the crucial one, because it is through that step that the broader situation and strategy of the organization shape the way in which quality improvement is approached. The initial purpose is usually taken from the larger context. Further, we have suggested that that key first step usually embodies – explicitly or implicitly – some mixture of the following basic purposes:

1 increasing producer quality by increasing the degree of internal control that management can exert over other groups/processes within the organization;

2 increasing the satisfaction of the end users of the service (user quality);
3 enhancing the democratic legitimacy of a particular government or institution by convincing the citizens that genuine efforts are being made to provide services which are directed at increasing their welfare yet are efficiently and fairly run.

A word of interpretative warning may be useful at this point. It may sound as though we believe in a rational world where all public service organizations choose explicit strategies after careful appraisals of their circumstances, and then proceed to design a quality improvement process that will dovetail neatly with the all-encompassing strategy. Some such organizations may exist, but if so, we have not come across many of them (though we have come across a few whose top managers *talk* as though that is what they are doing!). In fact we are quite sceptical of the strategy-making framework *as a description of everyday organizational reality*. It is not, for us, an empirically accurate model: on the contrary, we are familiar with certain public service organizations, large and small, which effectively have no strategy, but rather muddle along from month to month, reacting to each new government policy or managerial fashion or changed environmental circumstance is an essentially *ad hoc* manner. The point here is that in our model circumstances represent the *structure* of the situation while *strategy* represents human *agency*. It may be that in a given case the agency is vacillating or indistinct: it does not *have* to be purposeful, rational and so on. In such cases we would simply expect the structure to continue to exert its influences, that is circumstances would largely determine the kind of approach to quality improvement, if any, that took place. The organization concerned would drift into a particular kind of quality effort, instead of consciously choosing one. Whether most organization *actually* drift, or choose, and on what criteria they choose, are, of course, empirical questions.

Our own research and reading tend to suggest that strategies *are* often consciously chosen, but that the choice is frequently made as a reaction to somewhat adverse circumstances. Strategic reappraisals (and the adoption of major new approaches to quality such as TQM or benchmarking) often seem to take place when an organization recognizes that its environment has become very threatening. Perhaps competition has stiffened, or a hitherto monopolistic public service organization is now being exposed to competition for the first time. Perhaps an organization has suffered some sort of scandal or disaster and finds itself with a pressing need to restore its legitimacy. Perhaps it faces a technological revolution which is undermining its traditional mode of production. Furthermore it is not uncommon for such organizational traumas to be accompanied by a change of leadership, and a new man or woman at the top may bring in new strategic ideas. Radically changing circumstances invite, almost demand, some conscious reappraisal of what an organization is doing, but they do not usually dictate a single answer or solution.

Organizational cultures also play a part here. Chapter 5 showed very clearly how a strong administrative/legal culture helped shape responses to growing external pressures. In terms of Figure 11.1 the culture is in the left-hand box – a particularly pervasive sort of circumstance. We will deal with it more fully in the next and final chapter.

Thus the relationships within our framework are intended to be understood as probabilistic: they are tendencies rather than simple mechanical connections. The culture and circumstances *constrain* but do not absolutely determine the strategy-makers. If the circumstances happen to be x, y, z then strategies of type p or q would 'fit' better than strategy n. However, the strategists may nevertheless choose strategy n: by doing so they simple increase the probability that the organization's circumstances will prevent the strategy from being fully realized, because it will be running against the grain of the situation. To choose strategy p or q would be to choose a higher probability of success. If you are rather short in stature and are determined on a successful career in sport it is probably – but not *certainly* – the case that archery or table tennis would be better strategic choices than basketball or the high jump.

Another important preliminary point concerns the *level of phenomena under analysis*. In some of our case studies the level at which analysis was pitched was quite local: in Chapter 8 for example it was a single ward in a particular hospital. In other cases the focus was mainly at the system level (Chapters 3 and 4), where what was under scrutiny was an entire system on interacting organizations and hierarchical levels. It is at this ('higher', more generalized) level that the analysis in this final section of Chapter 11 is pitched. Much of the immediately preceding discussion of the 'steps' was quite detailed and specific, but now we will be working mainly at the system level where descriptions of broad patterns and statements of general tendency are the currency of discourse.

The central questions, therefore, are: 'How do circumstances constrain strategy-makers in respect to their approaches to quality improvement?' and 'Which strategies seem most appropriate to which strategic purposes?'

The first key circumstance in Figure 11.1 is the degree of

competition within the system. Generally speaking, the more competition there is the more likely planned improvements in quality *or price* will seem relevant and essential to staff within the organization. An ethic of continuous improvement is easier to implant in an organization which already knows it must constantly upgrade its performance in order to keep up with rivals. For some products or services price may be the key variable but, for most of the kinds of service in which the public sector is engaged, quality improvement will also be crucial.

Equally, the existence of significant competition will alert management to the desirability of staying in close touch with the needs and wants of those who use or buy the service (users are by no means always the same as buyers, especially in the public sector). This is likely to incline management towards the choice of user (or purchaser) satisfaction as a central purpose, and therefore towards models of quality improvement which stress consultation with major stakeholders and comparisons with one's principal competitors.

Conversely, the absence of competition weakens the imperative for improvement and strengthens the hand of tradition. If and when quality improvement is consciously embarked upon it is more likely to be by choosing a 'producer quality' model. A classic case here would be the practice of acute medicine in public hospitals where, all over Europe, doctors have been slow to adopt modern quality improvement methods (Jost, 1990). In the UK National Health Service, for example, the medical profession has adopted a rather introverted and confidential system of local, internal peer review, whereas in the much more competitive US health care market Medicare has been able to establish a more transparent, external review process (Pollitt, 1993a).

The second key circumstance referred to in Figure 11.1 is the degree of external regulation/autonomy. Much of the literature on quality improvement in the private sector assumes the existence of a relatively autonomous firm, able, within a framework of company law, to decide its own strategy and put as much or as little effort into quality improvement as its top managers wish. Take, for example, the classic story of the pioneering of benchmarking as a radical quality tool by the Xerox Corporation (Camp, 1989). Yet this is not at all a typical position for a public service organization. Frequently public service organizations find themselves quite closely controlled, regulated or supervised by one or more superior tiers of authority. In the UK, for example, local authorities are rather tightly controlled by central government. Executive agencies are bound by their framework agreements with their parent departments, and are not free simply to decide to adopt a new strategy without extensive external consultations.

In situations of low or middling autonomy (high or middling regulation), quality improvement may well become a jointly determined activity, in which the goals of the superior and subordinate tiers of authority are not by any means necessarily identical. In the UK National Health Service, for example, central government has placed huge emphasis on the length of waiting lists and on minimum waiting times in outpatients as key indicators of quality of service. Not all hospitals, and certainly not all doctors and nurses, would agree with this emphasis. Many clinical staff argue that it is the quality of the care that is rendered that is crucial for most patients and that how long patients have to wait for that care is a secondary, though not insignificant, consideration. Indeed, some would go further and claim that the obsession with waiting lists has had perverse effects. What we are witnessing here is the ability of a superior authority (in this case central government) to impose its concepts and measures on the subordinate organizations (hospitals) which actually deliver the services. Where the superior authority is strong there may be a general tendency towards *control* rather than user satisfaction as the dominant feature of its strategy, though much depends on how and how strongly the superior authority is itself held to public account.

A final relevant aspect of organizational autonomy is the degree to which an organization is free to adjust its own internal structure. In some European public sectors this freedom has been markedly increased during the last decade. Traditionally all local service delivery units (hospitals, schools and so on) would be structured in the same way, with more or less identical functional divisions (personnel, finance and so on) and grades. These structures would be dictated by a superior level in the state structure – a local or regional authority, or a department of the central government. Nowadays, however, it is becoming common to grant local service delivery units considerable discretion to organize as they themselves see fit. This is important in a quality context because the more radical approaches to quality improvement often trigger realization of a need fundamentally to restructure the organization.

In the UK, for example, Post Office Counters Ltd introduced TQM and then, within a few years, realized that focusing on business *processes* was so important that they wanted to completely reconfigure their internal structure so that it was organized on process lines rather than by traditional functional departments. Thus, instead of the organization being structured into departments such as finance and operations it was henceforth to be structured into processes such as stock distribution or cash transfers. Each process could then be managed as a single, end-to-end activity, including planning, operations, finance, personnel and all other functions. Clearly, a change such as this counts as a strategic shift for the organization, but it will only be available as a strategy if the organization has sufficient freedom realistically to contemplate selecting and designing its own structures without undue interference from some superior level of bureaucracy.

Turning to the third type of circumstance identified in Figure 11.1, we may say that some of the basic characteristics of a service itself may make some approaches to quality improvement very difficult to apply (and others more technically and culturally appropriate). Certain of these characteristics are identified in the figure, and we will briefly consider each in turn here.

For some major public services intensive face-to-face interactions between service providers and service users are absolutely fundamental to the success or otherwise of the service. Most education, much health care and a considerable proportion of community care and personal social services fall in this category. In other areas, however, such contact is minimal or entirely absent (for example the issue of driving licences; monitoring air pollution; tax collection). As mentioned in Chapter 1, theorists have begun to use the term *co-production* to describe what happens in those services where intensive face-to-face contacts are central. The term 'co-production' is meant to express the idea that the success of such services depends on the actions and responses of *both* parties – provider and user – not simply upon what the provider does. The child in school has to want to learn. It is often (not always) crucial that the patient trusts the doctor and co-operates by taking the prescribed drugs or observing a recommended diet or regime of exercise. The criminal who is on probation has to believe in the possibility and desirability of 'going straight', or she or he is likely to lapse back into crime at the first opportunity.

The implications of co-production for quality improvement are quite profound. Strategies based solely on increasing producer quality through greater control of provider behaviour will have limited (though nonetheless possibly worthwhile) impacts. Deeper success is likely to depend on adopting strategies which directly influence users' attitudes and behaviours as well as those of the providers – in other words on strategies which give central place to users' concepts of quality, and therefore to user satisfaction.

Another aspect under the heading of service characteristics is that labelled in Figure 11.1 as 'degree of technicity'. Some services may be fairly 'low tech'. Conventional school teaching, for example, depends on a teacher in a classroom. The technology may be no more that paper and pencils. The situation is essentially very flexible: a teacher may decide on Monday evening to teach in a new way on Tuesday morning. In other service contexts, by contrast, the technology of service delivery may be fixed (at least in the short term), complex and therefore quite constraining. A pollution inspectorate may use certain equipment to sample the air. A fire brigade will be equipped with certain types of (often quite expensive) vehicle, breathing apparatus, pumps and so on. These technologies limit what can be done, and cannot themselves be changed overnight. Strategies for quality improvement need to take account of such technological factors as constraints, but also to identify crucial points in time at which the technology can be changed. For example, when British Airways and Air France found themselves obliged to fly the Concorde airliner their choice of quality strategy was severely limited. They could hardly opt for an 'environmentally conscious' concept of quality since the aircraft they had to operate was, by contemporary standards, both extremely noisy and thirsty for fuel. Thus a 'high-speed luxury' concept of quality was the obvious one to adopt. Even the 'luxury' component was quite difficult to realize, since the Concorde design possessed quite a narrow, cramped fuselage. Luxury could only be achieved by creating space at the cost of what was (by the standards of other aircraft then entering service) a very low number of passengers per flight.

A less dramatic example of the importance of technological factors would be the modernization of social security payment systems. Making millions of social security transfer payments is an activity central to any modern welfare state. Precisely how this is done depends on the available and chosen technology, and certainly impacts on user satisfaction. Can payments be made directly into citizens' bank accounts, or do claimants have to made a trip to an office to queue for attention? How quickly does the payment come through once the amount of benefit has been assessed? Does the technology automatically provide the citizen-user with a printout of the same information as is available to the managers and clerical staff in the benefits agency, or is certain information denied to the citizen on grounds of confidentiality? There are even physical considerations such as whether the VDUs on the desks of benefit agency staff can be rotated so that the citizen-claimants can see the information displayed as well as the staff. Updating a system such as this (usually country-wide) is not only a major investment, but also a major opportunity for user participation – though in practice that opportunity is by no means always either offered (by the state) or taken (by the citizens or their representatives).

A third aspect under the heading of service characteristics is the extent to which a particular activity involves social ordering as well as straightforward service provision (the ordering/provision distinction was discussed in Chapter 1). Agreeing fundamental purposes and establishing a widely shared concept of quality can be especially challenging when the social ordering component is high. Consider the case of the prison service. In many countries the degree of social consensus over the purposes of imprisonment is not very impressive. Some groups see prison as primarily punitive: individuals who have transgressed should be denied the pleasures and privileges of normal society. Others see prisons as mainly to do with public safety: keeping dangerous criminals locked up. Others still believe that the main purpose of a prison service should be to rehabilitate so that those who have offended can be brought to see the error of their ways and provided with the skills and attitudes necessary to re-enter normal society at the earliest possible opportunity. What may be regarded as a 'quality prison' will vary very much according to which of these purposes is given the greatest priority.

Many social ordering functions share the characteristics that their real 'customers' are not so much the people they deal with (criminals, polluters, street demonstrators, hang-gliding enthusiasts) as the citizenry at large. It is presumed that the majority of citizens want criminals caught, air and water kept clean, peaceful public demonstrations and safe hang-gliding. In practice, however, the bulk of the citizenry may give very little thought indeed to these matters – unless and until something goes wrong that affects them personally (an escaped prisoner breaks into their house; a son or daughter is badly injured in a hang-gliding accident). So the signals coming from the community about what sort of service it wants may be very weak, very vague or very biased (towards the small minority who have recently and directly suffered from some negative occurrence). A strategic issue for social ordering services, therefore, is how it is to initiate and maintain a dialogue with citizens as to what kind of service they desire. (In a traditional bureaucratic culture this problem is simply avoided: the service providers just take their instructions from senior professionals and, beyond them, political leaders.)

The final circumstance in Figure 11.1 which is likely to shape organizational strategies is the obvious (but nonetheless occasionally overlooked) one of previous experience. One recent investigation into the grass-roots impact of citizens' charters seemed to indicate that one of the most significant factors in different organizations' experience of charter initiatives was the extent to which the particular organizational unit already had some record of trying to implement systematic approaches to defining and measuring standards of service (Beale and Pollitt, 1994). Basically, the earliest part of the learning curve was the steepest. Once an organization had learned to use one systematic approach it became that much easier to adapt to another one. Slowest progress tended to take place where quality issues had hitherto been largely implicit, informal and undiscussed. It was here that the investments of time, resources and training needed to be the greatest.

It would be possible to elaborate this analysis of organizational circumstances still further, but we hope we have done enough to demonstrate the shaping and constraining impact which some circumstances may exert on organizational strategies, and through them upon the more detailed steps organizations may take towards quality improvement. It must be emphasized that these relationships are not yet well researched and precisely documented. Rather they are tentative and hypothetical, though supported and illustrated by a range of reports, evaluations and case studies.

In conclusion, therefore, we advance some general propositions which seem to emerge from the consideration of cases and the broader analysis of strategies.

First, organizations which experience medium or high levels of competition are likely to be more receptive towards attempts at systematic quality improvement than monopolistic bureaucracies. Furthermore such organizations are more likely to appreciate the need for strategies oriented towards user satisfaction rather than producer control.

Secondly, organizations which experience a high degree of control and regulation from a superior authority are likely to be rather difficult places to launch 'home grown' quality initiatives. They are organizations where the staff are imbued with a culture of always 'looking over their shoulders' or 'up the line' rather than acting in the independent, creative way that many current techniques for quality improvement envisage. More likely such subordinate organizations will be forced to adopt particular quality systems by their superior authority. Internal management will then be faced with the considerable difficulty of winning staff support for what may well be seen as a new system imposed by the superior authority for its own purposes. In other words local 'ownership' of the quality improvement scheme is likely to be difficult to achieve. For this reason it would appear sensible for superior authorities, if they do insist on the introduction of a quality improvement scheme, to offer subordinate agencies as much freedom as possible to design and develop that scheme internally. Possibly, for example, the superior authority would simply specify steps 1 and 2 in our quality model, and leave management in the subordinate agency to work out the remaining steps for themselves.

Thirdly, organizations with highly diverse user groups and/or a high degree of co-production are likely to be especially challenging places to begin quality improvement. Their services are less likely to be standardized, and judgements about the value and purpose of these services may be quite varied. A strategy focused on producer quality may seem tempting to top management (because it avoids the complications of consulting multiple stakeholders) but in the long run such strategies are also likely to be fairly limited in their effects. Strategies focused on user satisfaction hold larger promise but will take considerable time and resources, especially if there is no history of that kind of exercise in the organization concerned previously. Techniques such as multi-stakeholder analysis (Backoff and Nutt, 1988) or, more radically, fourth-generation evaluation (Guba and Lincoln, 1989) may well be appropriate. In such circumstances a 'quick fix' simply is not available, which may be frustrating, especially for politicians.

Fourthly, the higher the degree of 'technicity' of a service, the less relevant some generic approaches to quality improvement may seem and the more a tailor-made approach may be needed. *If* other organizations which employ a similar technology can be found (even if they are in another sector) then functional benchmarking may be a possibility. Equally, however, whenever a service with a high technical content changes its technology (such as by changing its computer system) then a major opportunity for quality improvement is presented. Unfortunately, in the past some public services have regarded technological change of this kind as a purely internal, technical exercise, to be left entirely in the hands of technical experts and cost accountants.

Fifthly, the choice between user satisfaction strategies and producer quality strategies is connected to wider issues of legitimacy and democratic governance. In a *public* service, financed by the citizens' taxes and ostensibly working for the community at large, the arguments for giving weight to the views of those citizens receive an extra impetus. Consulting citizens may be a more complex and challenging process than 'market testing' the potential consumers for a new type of toothpaste, but it is also a richer and more socially integrative one. Indeed the currently fashionable quest for 'quality' services has already served – sometimes consciously, sometimes unwittingly – to reopen fundamental democratic questions of legitimacy, accountability and participation. It is appropriate that our final chapter should reflect further on the relationships between these fundamental issues and the quality of public services.

12

Concluding Reflections

Geert Bouckaert

Public sector quality is necessary for a legitimate government. At the same time, it seems to be impossible, intangible, opaque, ambiguous and multi-dimensional. If something is necessary and impossible at the same time, it becomes a challenge for policy and management.

The need to shift toward a multi-polar concept of quality results in a range of quality definitions, purposes, measures and indicators, and of improvement strategies. The choices of focusing on producer quality or user satisfaction, or legitimacy of the organization's authority, lead towards alternative improvement strategies. The case studies in this book suggest that a formal ten-step model of improvement is a useful framework within which to analyse the actual practice of improvement. We have also shown the importance of organizational circumstances in shaping organizational strategies towards quality improvement (see Chapter 11).

Another key circumstance is the political tradition and administrative culture of a country. The cases from different European countries all show that quality is getting higher on national agendas. The cases in this book show changes in similar, yet sometimes slightly different directions and with differences in speed. The Anglo-Saxon, the Scandinavian, the Latin and the Germanic traditions shape the quality culture of each public sector. A major question, as the European Union develops, is whether these differences are withering away.

Quality improvement strategies

A critical overview of the literature and the case studies allows us to say that there are:

1 different qualities for different purposes (producer quality, consumer satisfaction, legitimacy);
2 different quality measures and indicators for different types of service;

Producer orientation

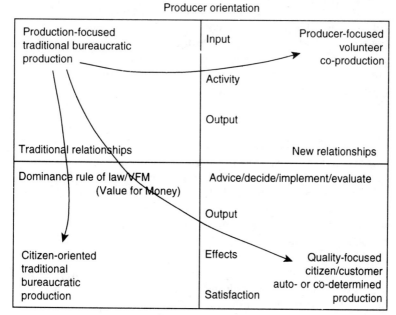

Figure 12.1   *The dynamics of quality improvement strategies*

3 different strategies of quality improvement for different purposes, services and circumstances.

This context fosters three rather distinctive development strategies, as detailed in the following sections (Figure 12.1).

From a producer-focused traditional bureaucracy to a producer-focused volunteer co-production or auto-production

Here the traditional bureaucracy keeps the responsibility for decision-making. The perception and focus of attention is producer determined and oriented towards the inside of the organization. Volunteers and customers are involved at different levels, but do not really change the balance of power. The major reason why the bureaucracy tolerates this improved position of the citizens is that the volunteers allow the hiving-off of tasks and the reduction of costs. Volunteers and citizens are used to maintain the level of service delivery at a reduced cost. A second reason may be to give citizens the illusion that they have a say in the production and distribution of goods and services. It is predominantly a cost-saving, illusory change. None of our particular cases could be situated in this category of change. Closest, perhaps, came the German case, where the *appearance* was one of decentralized, grass-roots democracy. In practice, however, there seems to have been little real citizen participation. In this respect it remained an illusory and rhetorical change.

From a producer-focused traditional bureaucracy to citizen-oriented traditional bureaucratic production

The traditional bureaucracy keeps the line of command and the relationships in place. Nevertheless, there is a growing focus on the customer and his or her needs and expectations. The traditional bureaucracy remains traditional but becomes open minded. This conservative change allows for the integration of survey information on expectations and satisfaction of customers. This information is processed in a traditional way and results in changes in policy. Part of the German and French tradition is represented here. Reference to the legal framework is important. The new perception of reality drives changes in practice inside the existing legal framework, or changes this framework better to correspond to fast-changing and differentiated situations and citizen groups. Respect for legality is the bottom line for this conservative change.

From a producer-focused traditional bureaucracy to quality-oriented citizen and customer auto-determination or co-determination of production

This trajectory of change is fundamental. The focus of attention includes the customer and his or her needs, expectations and satisfaction, and the related effects and outcomes. It also implies that new types of relationships are accepted. The citizen as citizen or customer or user of services becomes an active partner in the decision-making process. He or she, individually or as a group, shares responsibility at the level of advice or consultation, decision-making, implementation and evaluation. The quality agenda is combined with new patterns in sharing responsibility and account-ability, resulting in a renewed democracy. The Swedish tradition of decentralization, and the British tradition of limited legal frameworks and flexible implementation, create an environment that at least has *potential* for realizing this kind of development.

The precise location along this line of evolution is determined by the administrative culture, tradition, legal frameworks, type of service and level of government.

This change is fundamental because the shift in power is real, not an illusion. There is some transfer of competence to a new actor, the citizen as a customer. The citizen's new role may be more or less extensive. It may include participation in advice, decision-making, implementation and/or evaluation. This shift results in new patterns of responsibility and accountability. This progressive change gets new actors involved, first in an *ad hoc* way, then in a systematic way, and finally in a systemic way. The new actors become part of the systemic procedures. This results in new forms of democracy.

Strategies in the case studies

Looking again at the locations of the cases in this book it is obvious that they are all on or around the basic trend of fundamental change (Figure 12.2). Where the changes are only incremental, it is not always clear in what direction the evolution is going. The German and French traditions are more inclined towards conservative change which respects the legal tradition. Moving to a more fundamental change in perspective and relationship requires a deep, non-incremental change in their legal frameworks and thinking. The Scandinavian and British systems are more oriented to integrating new perceptions and relationships, because of the tradition of decentralization (Scandinavia) and the degrees of freedom of implementation (UK) in the existing systems.

Quality improvement in the National Logistic Command in the Netherlands (Nico Mol, Chapter 9) is determined by ISO and 'quality management by quality objectives', and process-determined quality as 'the whole of the attributes and characteristics of a product or service relevant to the fulfilment of stated or evident needs' is determined by NLC and its organizational units. These producers list the functional areas, identify priority result areas, specify perform-ance indicators and determine targets. Mol recognizes this is an inwardly focused activity, and that the needs and judgements of immediate clients (operational units) are only expressed in an indirect way.

Joss's pilot study on costing non-conformance at a UK National Health Service hospital (Chapter 8) refers explicitly to the cost of internal failure as determined by administrators, nurse managers and staff from the ward. These 'producers' determine what the conse-quences are of non-conformance to certain standard for a 'quality

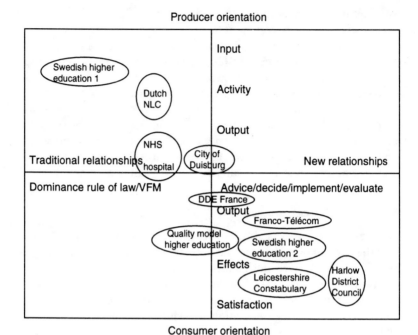

Figure 12.2   *Locating the case studies*

service' to patients. Although this case builds on traditional TQM elements (such as patient satisfaction, better information and improvement of amenities), Joss recognizes that the pilot study ignores the involvement of patients and carers, or other stakeholders. Quality criteria are professionally derived. The location of the pilot study (NHS hospital) is therefore in the upper left quadrant. The focus on cost and economy, and the implication of activity non-conformance for cost of output, put the case close to the border of the quadrant.

The Duisburg case (Klages, Chapter 5) is interesting because it shows how a legal tradition inhibits change, but also creates the framework for change. An awareness of the traditional focus on lawfulness and economy is crucial to understanding the German position and the direction of the change. Traditionally, quality assurance is guaranteed by the legal protection of civil rights and by civic participation. Formalized procedures of control will result in quality. The legal system was used to increase quality: first, access to administrative courts was improved; secondly, ombudsmen were created; thirdly, new laws guaranteed that citizens could use participatory procedures to be heard. Yet, a new ideal of responsiveness also entered the scene. The question became how to build societal acceptance regardless of the availability of legal justifications. This was an effort to weaken the legal tradition. At the same time, the co-operative state tried to tolerate 'informally' negotiated compromises without sacrificing the privilege of unilateral decision-making. In other words, there was an increased readiness to accept that outside definitions of quality would be taken into consideration in the process of decision-making. A critical screening showed that there initiatives did not result in a new type of quality-enforcing grass-roots democracy.

At present, in Duisberg, service standards are guaranteed by the dominating principle of the legal protection of civil rights. There are citizen offices and citizen bureaux which enable the citizen to address any civil servant who is present with any personal request. Finally, the *Verwaltungsrechtslehre* (academic discipline of administrative law) explores the possibilities of integrating a dialogical communication. The co-operative state investigates several approaches to joint public–private decision-making, which may even aim at interactively creating new norms and rules, which are appropriate to meet quality-oriented expectations from outside. Klages et al. recognize that this is still 'futuristic'.

In the French cases (Chapter 4), no unique quality model is imposed. Yet at the same time no quality programme will be approved without formal consultation with users. In general the quality programmes intend to create a balance between user expectations, the experience of professionals, cost constraints and specific objectives. Trosa's analysis sees that customer involvement will create the potential for new types of conflict with civil servants and politicians.

At the level of the DDEs in the Ministry of Equipment, the aim of developing indicators, as an aid to decision-making, is to motivate civil servants and to respond to decentralized demands. The focus on clients shifted from internal to elected officials, and in a third stage to direct users. The idea was to set up a recurrent dialogue to bring together user expectations and producer knowledge. This means that clients are consulted about desired outputs. At France-Télécom, quality indicators are determined by in-house personnel, mainly engineers. There is a unit that debates divergent interpretations of indicators and the board includes delegates of users and customers. It is only through representations to that board that users may determine and evaluate part of the outputs. Accountability is towards the board, then to the users. In terms of our diagram therefore the case is at the level of consumer-oriented outputs and advice as a new element of relationship. Télécom is slightly more to the right on the graph because customers seem to have more influence on decisions.

Van Vught and Westerheijden's model for quality assessment in higher education (Chapter 3) refers to intrinsic and extrinsic requirements. In their five-point scheme they refer to independent agents assessing at a meta level; self-evaluation, including external consultants; peer reviews with site visits; reporting of results; and indirect relationships between quality review and funding. This model relies heavily on producer-determined evaluations (internal or peer review). It also refers to consultation of clients (students), yet this is not really in an accountability context. Its focus potentially may extend beyond outputs to effect level. Therefore it is in the bottom left as well as in the bottom right quadrants in Figure 12.2. This is not a big surprise since the authors wanted to combine the most important elements of the British tradition (peer review by co-opted fellows) and the French tradition (accountability to external stake-holders).

The Swedish case on the quality pilot study in higher education (Westlund, Chapter 7) is ambiguous. On the one hand the case is very producer focused and is determined by a distant and strong bureaucracy. The producer-determined goals of the education system are taken for granted and left out of the discussion altogether. These goals are 'centrally given' and 'not changeable at the time'. These centrally prescribed goals exclude other goals, whether at the departmental or at the course level. This results in a position in the upper quadrant (Swedish higher education 1). On the other hand, there is an outcome focus, and actors include not just teachers and administrators, but also students and industry representatives. The focus is not just on resources and process but also on results. The information is used to influence the traditional decision-makers. Students and other stakeholders are surveyed to get more infor-mation. The stage of consultation and advice is not transcended. This results in a position in the bottom right quadrant (Swedish higher education 2). The reference to future studies implies that at a later stage there may be many fewer central directives, and those very general. A major concern will be to know how the customers' needs are converted into quality goals for every process, and what the degree of goal fulfilment is.

The case of the Leicestershire Constabulary (Hanney, Chapter 10) indicates fundamental changes in perception and relationships. The primacy of customer expectations and needs is established through public opinion surveys. This information is not just nice to know, but is used to measure performance against standards which reflect public expectations. This puts this case in the bottom right quadrant. Next to resources, activities and outputs, major attention is paid to effects and satisfaction. The level of involvement of citizens seems to be a consultative or advisory one, rather than co-decision or beyond.

The case of Harlow District Council, as described by Lucy Gaster (Chapter 6), is probably the most 'progressive' one in our collection. Neighbourhood offices attempt to provide more of what people want. The most important techniques to establish these new relationships are: first, the development of an external learning cycle through local knowledge; secondly, community development; and thirdly, new consultation mechanisms in area committees, for example. The Copernican change suffusing the new relationship is that the council is now working with people, 'not doing things to them'. This evidently took some time. The new patterns had to grow. Citizens first had to be heard, then to be involved, and finally to be empowered. The deepening of the levels of hearing, involving and empowering people shifted from decisions on definition, through monitoring, and finally to compliance (evaluation). This change was the result of converging and interlocking policies of decentralization and democratization, quality improvement and contract monitoring. These mechanisms of participative democracy are a dynamic involvement of users and residents because of the cyclical process of defining, monitoring and redefining quality in contracts. This puts the case almost in the bottom right of Figure 12.2.

Thus we have a 'geography' of case studies. The case studies may be mapped according to the two developmental dimensions: producer/consumer quality focus, and relational change. These two dimensions indicate an interaction between quality policy and new forms of democracy.

The dynamics of changing relationships

This location of cases allows the reader to map other quality improvement programmes and the direction in which organizations are evolving. Patterns of quality improvement can be related to organizational strategies. These strategies can be defined in terms of the following questions:

What are the values and purposes?
What are the rules for allocating resources?
What are the key structures and processes?
What are the internal regulation and monitoring systems?
What is the learning process?

The answers to these questions are influenced by the degree of competition, the degree of external regulation or autonomy, the service characteristics, and the extent of previous experience of systematic quality improvement (Figure 11.1). A crucial value assumption is the degree to which customers count in the perception of the service (output, effects, satisfaction), and in the functioning of the organization (customers as passive recipients which you can consult, or as active co-producers).

Major questions obviously arise from this kind of classification. Where, on Figure 12.2, is a given service currently located? Where should it be heading? How can management and other staff – and citizens – help shift it from here to there?

Challenges for the future

This book suggests that quality improvement in the public sector is not just a technical problem of measurement and implementation. It is also a political problem where changes in quality are bound up with the functioning of government and ultimately of society. Some of the cases described show clearly that quality improvement and new forms of democracy in society are converging and mutually reinforcing strategies of modernization. This results in several unresolved questions and many future challenges.

Values
The traditional bureaucracy derived its legitimacy from a hierarchy of values which stressed first legality, then equity, effectiveness and efficiency, and lastly economy. Some new types of public services procurement, through market mechanisms, almost reverse that order. The systemic order then becomes economy, efficiency, effectiveness, equity and lastly legality. None of our cases show this 'market state' philosophy in an ideal or pure form. Instead, our 'sample' exhibits attempts to try to keep legality as an important value, but to try also to improve the value status of effectiveness by

means of a quality focus which is guaranteed because of customer involvement. A major question is how legality and effectiveness are related and how this will affect efficiency and economy. In other words, what is the price to pay for a stronger quality focus and for these new forms of democracy?

Law
Legality and the legal framework become a crucial element in this discussion. The German example shows clearly that first there were efforts to improve quality with legal tools. Then there were some attempts to improve quality outside the legal framework up to the 'border of unlawful behaviour' (p. 71). The last stage described some attempts to renew the legal framework with a double intention: first, to keep valuable arrangements that protect the individual and civic rights; and secondly, to guarantee quality and citizen involvement to increase the legitimacy of the system. In effect there is an exploration of, on the one hand, the possibilities for integrating a 'dialogical' communication with citizens into the legal basis of administrative activity; and, on the other hand, the shift of laws and rules as preset frames interactively to create norms and rules which are appropriate to meet quality-oriented expectations from outside. These are two major evolutions which should modernize law as a tool for societal governance.

Two important aspects of law and its modernization are to be taken into account. First, there is the time dimension. It takes a lot of time to create new laws. Most of the time laws lag behind reality. In a stable and static society this causes minor frictional problems. In an unstable and dynamic society this causes chronic frictions. The decision to guide organizations by real-time monitoring systems and performance indicators instead of slowly changing laws and rules becomes problematic unless laws can be framed in forms which permit continuing adjustments in the light of an ongoing dialogue with partly unpredictable reality.

Secondly, there is the issue of generality. Laws are designed to cover the whole population, or groups or large categories of that population. To the extent that broad legal categories do not differentiate and do not match personalized necessities and circumstances, the law could come to be considered as an anti-quality, anti-effective tool for governance. Differentiation may have to be traded off against equity and equal treatment.

The more a country relies on law and the more it depends on this legal framework to improve service quality and effectiveness, the more that country will feel the necessity to modernize this legal framework. All European countries will have to take this required shift into account. However, contemporary approaches to service quality are increasingly couched in terms of responsiveness to *individual* wants and needs. The challenge will be to reshape law to accommodate or even enforce the 'new relationships'. To strengthen quality in the public sector, the citizen as an actor may need a protected set of rights within a renewed form of democracy.

Conflicts
The new customer-oriented focus on quality, satisfaction and effectiveness together with the possibility of a related and reinforcing involvement of empowered citizens creates additional potential sources of conflict. First, there is a potential friction with civil servants, professionals and their trade unions. They know their job because they have been doing this for so long, and cannot accept that 'outsiders' and people ignorant of 'technical' or 'professional' standards are going to co-decide, let alone co-implement or co-evaluate. Secondly, managers, though until now gainers from the 'new public management', may find even their freedom of action limited by greater citizen empowerment. 'Consultation' is one thing, co-determination another. Thirdly, there is also potential friction with politicians. Our present system of democracy relies on mandates and delegation to (professional) politicians. Direct citizen involvement is a short-cut in traditional democratic procedures. It may well represent a relative loss of power for traditional politicians. Thus new forms of democracy are a challenge for our traditional procedural democracies. These new forms will have to be made explicit. The active citizen as an institutionalized and systemic actor will need to learn new patterns of decision-making, of responsibility-sharing, and of accountability. Procedures for conflict resolution will no doubt also require modification. All this could not be accomplished in a single year, or even a decade.

Transferability
A fourth challenge is that of transferring good practice between types of service, between levels of government, and between different countries and different administrative cultures. Transferring good practice, in general, requires an organizational strategy. One of the dynamic components of such a strategy is the individual and organizational learning capacity.

In this context, one could ask what the implications are of a competitive European public sector which may result in a converging vision of quality, possibly even a common quality policy in Europe. The German case indicated that the 'German model is fading away', and that they are importing elements from other countries. Citizen or customer charters first appeared in the UK and then in France, Belgium and Portugal. The effort to look for the best practice and the highest quality in the public sector is organized in contests and competitions with awards such as charter marks in different European countries. The European Foundation on Quality Management has created a homogeneous platform for both public and private sectors, right across Europe. The OECD has begun to discuss the scope for the international benchmarking of public services. All these initiatives show a common concern, apply similar methods and techniques, follow analogous conceptual frameworks. Is this too much of a reduction of the complexity of reality? Is this standardization of quality facilitating the learning cycle? Is this common learning cycle going to facilitate the transferability of good quality practice?

Most of these initiatives consider the quality problem from a technical point of view. It is about measurement, motivation, organizational features and focus or perception. This book argues that new societal relationships, where the citizen as a customer is involved in or even committed to the political framework, are ultimately as or more important than the technics of quality. Issues of trust and participation are as salient as those of measurement and resourcing. It would be strange indeed if, amidst all the attention being given to quality processes, the democratic process itself was to escape our reforming zeal.

References

ACPO (1990) *Setting the Standards for Policing: Meeting Community Expectation.* London: Association of Chief Police Officers.

ACPO (1992) *The Police Service: Performance Indicators.* Quality of Service Committee, London: Association of Chief Police Officers.

Alvesson, M. (1987) *Organization Theory and Technocratic Conciousness: Rationality, Ideology and Quality of Work.* Berlin: de Gruyter.

Ammons, D. (1984) *Municipal Productivity, A Comparison of Fourteen High-Quality Service Cities.* New York: Praeger.

Atkinson, P. (1990) *Creating Culture Change: the Key to Successful Total Quality Management.*

Backoff, R. and Nutt, P. (1988) 'A process for strategic management with specific application for the non-profit organization', in J. Bryson and R. Einsweiler (eds), *Strategic Planning: Threats and Opportunities for Planners.* Chicago: Planners Press.

Ball, C. (1985) *Fitness for Purpose.* Guildford: SRHE and NFER-Nelson.

Beale, V. and Pollitt, C. (1994) 'Charters at the grassroots: a first report', *Local Government Studies*, 20(2): 202–25.

Birnbaum, R. (1989) 'The quality cube: how college presidents assess quality', in *Quality in the Academic: Proceedings from a National Symposium.* National Center for Postsecondary Governance and Finance, University of Maryland.

Blackman, T. (1992) 'Improving quality through research', in I. Sanderson (ed.), *Management of Quality in Local Government.* Harlow: Longman.

Blankart, C. (1987) 'Limits to privatization', *European Economic Review*, 31: 346–51.

Bouckaert, Geert (1991) 'Public productivity in retrospective', in Marc Holzer (ed.), *Public Productivity Handbook.* New York: Marcel Dekker Inc. pp. 15–46.

Bouckaert, Geert (1993) 'Measurement and meaningful management', *Public Productivity and Management Review*, XVII(I): 31–43.

Bouckaert, Geert (1995) 'Improving performance measurement', in A. Halachmi and G. Bouckaert (eds), *The Enduring Challenges in Public Management: Surviving and Excelling in a Changing World.* San Francisco: Jossey-Bass.

Bradford, D., Malt, R. and Oates, W. (1969) 'The rising cost of local public services; some evidence and reflections', *National Tax Journal*, XXII(2): 185–202.

Brennan, J. (1990) 'Quality assessment in the public sector in Great Britain', in L. Goedegebuure, P. Maassen and D. Westerheijden (eds), *Peer Review and Performance Indicators.* Utrecht: Lemma.

Brennan, J., Goedegebuure, L., Shah, T., Westerheijden, D. and Weusthof, P. (1992) *Towards a Methodology for Comparative Quality Assessment in European Higher Education.* London: CNAA, CHEPS, HIS.

Brookes, S. (1991) 'Taking account of the consumer'. Unpublished dissertation, Polytechnic of Wales.

Brunel University (1993) *The Valuation of Changes in Quality in the Public Services: Report Prepared for H.M. Treasury by Brunel University*. London: HMSO.

Butler, A. (1992a) 'Developing quality insurance in police services', *Public Money and Management*, 12: 23–7.

Butler, A. (1992b) *Police Management* (2nd edn.). Aldershot: Dartmouth.

Camp, R. (1989) *Benchmarking: the Search for Industry Best Practices that Lead to a Superior Performance*. Milwaukee: Quality Press.

Carter, N., Klein, R. and Day, P. (1992) *How Organisations Measure Success: the Use of Performance Indicators in Government*. London: Routledge.

Cave, M., Hanney, S., Kogan, M. and Trevett, G. (1988) *The Use of Performance Indicators in Higher Education*. London: Kingsley.

Cazenave, P. (1990) 'France', in H. Kells (ed.), *The Development of Performance Indicators for Higher Education: a Compendium for Eleven Countries*. Paris: OECD.

CEC (1991) *Memorandum on Higher Education in the European Community*. Brussels: Commission of the European Communities.

CEPPP (1992) *Considering Quality: an Analytical Guide to the Literature on Quality and Standards in the Public Services*. Uxbridge: Centre for the Evaluation of Public Policy and Practice, Brunel University.

CEPPP (1994) *An Evaluation of Total Quality Management in the National Health Service: Synopsis of the Final Report to the Department of Health*. Uxbridge: Centre for the Evaluation of Public Policy and Practice, Brunel University.

Clapham, D. (1993) 'Evaluation and assessment of performance', in N. Thomas, N. Deakin and J. Doling (eds), *Learning from Innovation: Housing and Social Care in the 1990s*. Birmingham: Birmingham Academic Press, pp. 105–22.

Clark, B. (1983) *The Higher Education System: Academic Organization in Cross-National Perspective*. Berkeley: University of California Press.

Crosby, P. (1979) *Quality is Free*. New York: McGraw-Hill.

Crosby, P. (1988) *The Eternally Successful Organization*. New York: McGraw-Hill.

CVCP (1985) *Report of the Steering Committee for Efficiency Studies in Universities* (the Jarratt Report). London: Committee of Vice Chancellors and Principals.

CVCP (1987) *Performance Indicators in Universities: a Second Statement by the Joint CVCP/UGC Working Group*. London: Committee of Vice Chancellors and Principals.

CVCP/UGC (1987) *University Management Statistics and Performance Indicators*. London: Committee of Vice Chancellors and Principals and University Grants Committee.

CVCP/UGC (1989) *University Management Statistics and Performance Indicators in the UK*. London: Committee of Vice Chancellors and Principals and University Grants Committee.

Day, P. and Klein, R. (1987) *Accountabilities: Five Public Services*. London: Tavistock.

Deming, W. (1986) *Out of the Crisis*. Boston: MIT.

DES (1991) *Higher Education: a New Framework*. London: HMSO.

Dochy, F., Segers, M. and Wijnen, W. (1990a) 'Selecting performance indicators: a proposal as a result of research', in L.C.J. Goedegebuure, P.A.M. Maassen and D.F. Westerheijden (eds), *Peer Review and Performance Indicators*. Utrecht: Lemma.

Dochy, F., Segers, M. and Wijnen, W. (eds) (1990b) *Management Information and Performance Indicators in Higher Education: an International Issue*. Assen/Maastricht: Van Gorcum.

Edwardsson, B., Thomasson, B. and Øvretveit, J. (1994) *Quality of Service: Making it Really Work*. London: McGraw-Hill.

Ellwein, T. and Hesse, J. (1987) *Das Regierungssytem der Bundesrepublik Deutschland* (6th edn). Opladen: Westdeutscher.

Findlay, P. (1990) 'Developments in the performance indicator debate in the United Kingdom: the research project at Portsmouth Polytechnic', in L. C. J. Goedegebuure, P. A. M. Maassen and D. F. Westerheijden (eds), *Peer Review and Performance Indicators*. Utrecht: Lemma.

Fukuhara, R. (1977) *Productivity Improvement in Cities*. Municipal Yearbook. Washington DC: ICMA.

Gaster, L. (1992) 'Quality, devolution and decentralisation', in I. Sanderson (ed.), *Management for Quality in Local Government*, Warwick Series in Local Economic and Social Strategy. Harlow: Longmans.

Gaster, L. (1993) 'Neighbourhood centres and community care in Liverpool', in R. Smith et al. (eds), *Working Together for Better Community Care*, SAVS Study. Bristol: School for Advanced Urban Studies.

Grizzle, G. (1981) 'A manager's guide to the meaning and uses of performance measurement', *American Review of Public Administration*, 15(1): 16–28.

Grossman, H. (ed.) (1971) *Bürgerinitiativen: Schritte zur Veränderung?* Frankfurt am Main: Campus.

Grunow, D. (1988) *Bürgernache Verwaltung: Theorie, Empirie, Praxismodelle*. Frankfurt/New York: Campus.

Guba, E. and Lincoln, Y. (1989) *Fourth Generation Evaluation*. Newbury Park, CA: Sage.

Guin, J. (1990) 'The reawakening of higher education in France', *European Journal of Education*, 25.

Gummesson, E. (1993) *Quality in Service Organization*. Stockholm: ISQA.

Hart, M. (1994) 'Improving the quality of outpatient services in NHS hospitals: some policy considerations', paper presented at the EGPA Annual Conference in Bad Tatzmansdorf, Austria, 20–23 September.

Hatry, H. (1979) *Efficiency Measurement for Local Government Services: Some Initial Suggestions*. Washington DC: The Urban Institute.

Hatry, H. and Fisk, D. (1971) *Improving Productivity and Productivity Measurement in Local Governments*. Washington DC: The Urban Institute.

Hatry, H., Blair, L., Fisk, D., Greiner, J., Hall, J. and Schaenman, P. (1992) *How Effective are your Community Services: Procedures for Measuring their Quality*. Washington DC: Urban Institute & ICMA.

Hayes, F. (1977) *Productivity in Local Government*. Lexington, MA: Lexington Books.

Hill, H. (1993) 'Staatskommunikation: Begriff, Erschelnungsformen und Entwicklungschancen', *VOP*, 5: 285–8.

Hirst, M. (1991) 'What do we mean by quality?', *Policing*, 7: 183–93.

HMIC (1991) *Quality of Service: a Framework of Performance Indicators*. Her Majesty's Inspectorate of Constabulary, London: Home Office.

Home Office (1983) Manpower, Effectiveness and Efficiency in the Police Service, Circular 114/1983.

Home Office (1990) *Victim's Charter*. London: Home Office.

Home Office (1992) *Circular 40/1992*. London: Home Office.

Home Office (1993) *Police Reform: a Police Service for the Twenty-First Century*. Cm. 2281. London: HMSO.

Johnes, J. and Taylor, J. (1990) *Performance Indicators in Higher Education: UK Universities*. Buckingham: Open University/SRHE.

Joint Consultative Committee (1990) *Operational Policing Review*. London: Joint Consultative Committee.

Jones, S. and Levi, M. (1982) 'Police–public relationships: a study of the police and the public's perceptions of each other', mimeo, University College, Cardiff.

Jones, S. and Levi, M. (1983) 'The police and the majority: the neglect of the obvious', *Police Journal*, LVI: 4, October.

Jones, S. and Silverman, E. (1984) 'What price efficiency? Circular arguments: financial constraints on the Police in Britain', *Policing*, 1(1): 31–48.

Joss, R., Kogan, M. and Henkel, M. (1992) *Evaluation of Total Quality Management in the NHS: Second Interim Report to the Department of Health*. Uxbridge: Centre for the Evaluation of Public Policy and Practice/Brunel University.

Jost, T. (1990) *Assuring the Quality of Medical Practice: an International Comparative Study*. London: King's Fund Project Paper 2.

Juran, J. (1988) *Juran on Planning for Quality*. New York: Free Press.

Kells, H. (ed.) (1990) *The Development of Performance Indicators for Higher Education: a Compendium for Eleven Countries*. Paris: OECD.

Kells, H. (1992) 'An analysis of the nature and recent development of performance indicators in higher education', *Higher Education Management*, 4: 131–8.

Kinserdal, L. and Ströberg, L. (1991) *Concentration and Profile* (in Swedish).

Klages, H. and Haubner, O. (1995) 'Strategies for public sector modernization', in G. Bouckaert and A. Halachmi (eds), *The Enduring Challenges in Public Management: Surviving and Excelling in a Changing World*. San Francisco: Jossey-Bass.

Kogan, M. (1991) 'Policy making and evaluation in higher education', *Higher Education Policy*, 3(4): 30–2.

Le Grand, J. and Bartlett, W. (1993) *Quasi-Markets and Social Policy*. Basingstoke: Macmillan.

Leicestershire Constabulary (1991) 'A report prepared for the Chief Constable's Meeting Community Expectations Seminar', mimeo, Leicestershire Constabulary, Leicester.

Leicestershire Constabulary (1993) *Policing Charter: Meeting Community Expectations*. Leicester: Leicestershire Constabulary.

Lenk, K. (1990) *Nueue Informationdlenste im Verhaltnis von Bürger und Verwaltung*. Heidelberg: Decker und Mueller.

Linke, R. (1992) 'Some principles for application of performance indicators in higher education', *Higher Education Management*, 4: 194–203.

Lipsky, M. (1980) *Street-Level Bureaucracy*. New York: Russell Sage Foundation.

Lucier, P. (1992) 'Performance indicators in higher education: lowering the tension of the debate', *Higher Education Management*, 4: 204–14.

Middaugh, M. and Hollowell, D. (1992) 'Developing appropriate measures of academic and administrative productivity as budget support data for resource allocation decisions', *Higher Education Management*, 4: 164–78.

MOW (1985) *Hoger Onderwijs: Autonomie en Kwaliteit*. Ministerie voor Onderwijsen Wetenschappen.

Neave, M. (1991) *Models of Quality Assurance in Europe*. London: CNAA.

OPCS (1993) *British Crime Survey*. London: OPCS/HMSO.

Orwell, G. (1949) *Nineteen Eighty-Four*. London: Secker and Warburg.

Pirsig, R. (1974) *Zen and the Art of Motorcycle Maintenance*. Morrow: New York.

Pitschas, R. (1990) *Verwaltungverantwortung und Verwaltungsverfahren.* Münich: C. H. Beck.

Pollitt, C. (1990) 'Performance indicators: root and branch', in M. Cave, M. Kogan and R. Smith (eds), *Output and Performance Measurement in Government: the State of the Art.* London: Jessica Kingsley, pp. 167–78.

Pollitt, C. (1993) 'The struggle for quality: the case of the National Health Service', *Policy and Politics*, 21(3): 161–70.

Pollitt, C. (1993a) 'The politics of medical quality: auditing doctors in the UK and the USA', *Health Services Management Research*, February, 6 (1): 24–94.

Pollitt, C. (1994) 'The Citizen's Charter: a preliminary analysis', *Public Money and Management*, 14(2): 1–5.

Popper, K. (1957) *The Poverty of Historicism.* London: Routledge and Kegan Paul.

Popper, K. (1983) *Realism and the Aim of Science* (ed. W. W. Bartley III). Hutchinson: London.

Prime Minister (1991) *The Citizen's Charter: Raising the Standard*, Cm 1599, July. London: HMSO.

Prior, D., Stewart, J. and Walsh, K. (1993) *Is the Citizen's Charter a Charter for Citizens?*, The Belgrave Papers 7, London: Local Government Management Board.

Reinermann, H. (1986) *Verwaltungsinnovation und Informationsmanagement: 92 Thesen zur Bewältigung der informationstechnischen herausforderung.* Heidelberg: Decker und Mueller.

Robertson Bell Associates (1993) *The Presentation of Citizen's Charter Indicators: Research Carried Out for the Audit Commission and Epsom and Ewell Borough Council.* Leeds: Robertson Bell Associates.

Rosen, E. (1984) 'Productivity: concepts and measurement', in M. Holzer and S. Nagels (eds), *Productivity and Public Policy.* Beverly Hills: Sage.

Ross, J. and Burkhead, J. (1974) *Productivity in the Local Government Sector.* Lexington: Lexington Books, D. C. Heath and Co.

Scharpf, F. (1970) *Demokratietheorie Zwischen Utopie und anpassung.* Konstanz: Universitätsverlag.

SIQ (1993) *The Swedish Quality Award* (in Swedish). Swedish Institute for Quality Development.

Sizer, J. (1990) 'Funding councils and performance indicators in quality assessment in the United Kingdom', in L.C.J. Goedegebuure, P.A.M. Maassen and D.F. Westerheijden (eds), *Peer Review and Performance Indicators.* Utrecht: Lemma.

Sizer, J. (1992) 'Performance indicators in government – higher institutions relationships: lessons for government', *Higher Education Management*, 4: 156–63.

Sizer, J., Spee, A. and Bormans, R. (1992) 'The role of performance indicators in higher education', *Higher Education*, 24: 133–55.

Spee, A. and Bormans, R. (1992) 'Performance indicators in government – institutional relations: the conceptual framework', *Higher Education Management*, 4: 139–55.

Staropoli, A. (1991) 'The French Comité National d'Évaluation', in A. Craft (ed.), *Quality Assessment in Higher Education.* London: Falmer.

Stewart, J. (1992) *Managing Difference: the Analysis of Service Characteristics.* Birmingham: Institute of Local Government Studies/Local Government Management Board.

Steward, J. and Ranson, S. (1994) *Management for the Public Domain*, Basingstoke: Macmillan.

Stolte-Heiskanen, V. (1992) 'Research performance evaluation in the higher education sector: a grass-roots perspective', *Higher Education Management*, 4: 179–93.

Storey, J. (1989) 'Human resource management in the public sector', *Public Money and Management*, 9(3): 19–24.

van Vught, F. (ed.) (1989) *Governmental Strategies and Innovation in Higher Education*. London: Jessica Kingsley.

van Vught, F. (1991) 'Higher education quality assessment in Europe: the next step', *CRE-action*, 4: 61–82.

Vroeijenstijn, T. and Acherman, H. (1990) 'Control oriented versus improvement oriented quality assessment', in L.C.J. Goedegebuure, P.A.M. Maassen and D.F. Westerheijden (eds), *Peer Review and Performance Indicators*. Utrecht: Lemma.

VSNU (1988) *De Evaluatie van het Project Proefvisitaties*. Utrecht: VSNU.

VSNU (1990) *Guide for External Programme Review*. Utrecht: VSNU.

Wagener, F. (1969) *Neubau der Verwaltung*. Berlin: Duncker und Humblot.

Walsh, K. (1993) 'Contracts', in N. Thomas, M. Deakin and J. Doling (eds), *Learning from Innovation: Housing and Social Care in the 1990s*. Birmingham: Birmingham Academic Press.

Westerheijden, D. (1990) 'Peers, performance and power', in L.C.J. Goedegebuure, P.A.M. Maassen and D.F. Westerheijden (eds), *Peer Review and Performance Indicators*. Utrecht: Lemma.

Westerheijden, D., Weusthof, P. and Frederiks, M. (1992) 'Effects of self-evaluations and visiting committees', paper presented at the Fourth International Conference on Assessing Quality in Higher Education, Enschede, 28–30 July.

Westlund, J. (1991) *A Study for Evaluating the Education in General Business Economics* (in Swedish). Göteborg: University of Göteborg.

Williams, P. (1991) *The CVCP Academic Audit Unit*. Birmingham: CVCP.

Williamson, C. (1992) *Whose Standards? Consumer and Professional Standards in Health Care*. Buckingham: Open University Press.

Wilson, J. (1989) Bureaucracy: *What Government Agencies do and Why they do it*. New York.

Wipfler, J. (1979) *Leitfaden der Verwaltungslehre*. Berlin: Duncker & Humblot.

Yorke, M. (1990) 'Performance indicators: towards a synoptic framework', paper presented at EAIR, Lyon, 9–12 September.

Young, D. (1990) 'The Academic Audit Unit: an organization for university quality management', in L. C. J. Goedegebuure, P. A. M. Maassen and D. F. Westerheijden (eds), *Peer Review and Performance Indicators*. Utrecht: Lemma.

Zeithmel, V., Parasuraman, A. and Berry, L. (1990) *Delivery Quality Service*. New York: Free Press.

Index